Awe and Expectation

Awe and Expectation

On Being Stewards of the Gospel

ALLEN G. JORGENSON

WIPF & STOCK · Eugene, Oregon

AWE AND EXPECTATION
On Being Stewards of the Gospel

Copyright © 2010 Allen G. Jorgenson. All rights reserved. Except for brief quotations in critical publications or reviews, no part of this book may be reproduced in any manner without prior written permission from the publisher. Write: Permissions, Wipf and Stock Publishers, 199 W. 8th Ave., Suite 3, Eugene, OR 97401.

Wipf & Stock
An Imprint of Wipf and Stock Publishers
199 W. 8th Ave., Suite 3
Eugene, OR 97401

www.wipfandstock.com

ISBN 13: 978-1-60608-795-4

Manufactured in the U.S.A.

To my mother and father
(requiescat in pace),
who together
taught me to live
in awe and expectation

Contents

Preface • ix

Acknowledgments • xi

1. Sacramental Stewardship • 1
2. Stewardship, Justification, and Justice • 16
3. Stewardship and Fundraising • 30
4. The Praying Steward • 49
5. Stewarding the Body • 69
6. Stewardship of Education: Teaching to Learn • 86
7. Proclaiming Stewardship and a Stewardship of Proclamation • 105

Afterword • 118

Bibliography • 121

Index • 125

Preface

Few would contend that stewardship is a neglected theme in most North American churches. The last three decades have witnessed a level of attentiveness to this subject unlike any other in the life of the average parish. After all, how many congregations set aside an Evangelism Month?

Yet the recent press of finances necessitates new attention to stewardship, in one mode or another. Many would assert that a certain malaise meets the annual visitation of this theme in the life of the average parish. Stewardship has become not so much a necessary evil as a banal good—which may be far worse. Why is this?

In part, I think it is because the practice of stewardship has been disconnected from a theology of stewardship. Aside from a handful of theological treatments (most notably Douglas John Hall's), stewardship is too often dealt with under the genre of "how to." In this book I argue that we experience the vigor of stewardship only as we connect stewardship to a theological treatment of broader practices of church life. Stewardship's vital signs are measured in its appearance in word and sacrament; in prayer and praise; in teaching and practising a passion for justice. In sum, the core practices of the church—those means by which God acts in and through us—shape, invigorate, and inform a theology of stewardship, and stewardship returns the favor. Certain contours of church life are visible only when we shine the light of stewardship on them.

That is what I purport to do in this book. I work with the premise that our identity as stewards shapes in us a posture of awe and expectation, the only antidote to the desperation that masquerades as inspiration in the lives of too many churches. I intend to demonstrate how the core practices of the church render us stewards of the gospel, and how these practices correspondingly shape our theology of stewardship. This, in turn, shapes our apprehension of these core practices.

After a glance at the table of contents, many readers will question why I have not included this or that practice in my overview of the interrelationship between stewardship and the church's core practices. I offer only this explanation to the disappointed reader: certain topics are missing because I do not consider them to be core practices of the church (such as, for instance, the use of seasons to order the church year), or because they are best dealt with by theologians with an expertise and sensitivity that exceeds my own (church architecture and congregational song come to mind), or because books are written only by sacrificing what is important—sometimes to their authors, sometimes to their readers, but hopefully never to the books themselves.

Acknowledgments

I AM PLEASED TO thank the many people who helped me in writing this book.

First, I thank Kay and Ken Jorgenson, my mother and father (the latter now in the cloud of witnesses). They taught me the joy of stewardship by living graciously and with kindness. To them I dedicate this book.

Second, I thank my colleagues and students at Waterloo Lutheran Seminary, who read some of these chapters and helped me think through the implications of the ideas I advance herein. I also thank Cheryl M. Peterson of Trinity Lutheran Seminary in Columbus, Ohio, whose reading of an earlier draft allowed me to improve the present text, and Anne Brennan, who carefully edited the final manuscript.

Thanks are due also to a number of people who engaged with this material in seminars I presented, enabling me to develop my appreciation for the importance of stewardship: the pastors of the Northern and Atlantic Conferences of the Eastern Synod of the Evangelical Lutheran Church in Canada (ELCIC); the pastors of the British Columbia Synod of the ELCIC; participants in the 2005 Return to Sender Conference of the Ontario Stewardship Network; participants in the 2006 Family Camp at Camp Kuriakos at Sylvan Lake, Alberta; and participants who joined Jeff Pym and me as together we learned about stewardship at the 2006 Luther Hostel held at Waterloo Lutheran Seminary.

I am also pleased to thank the Office of Research Services at Wilfrid Laurier University for a grant to aid in the preparation of this manuscript.

Finally, I thank my wife, Gwenanne, and my children, Anelise, Nadia, and Corin, for their constant support and encouragement.

1

Sacramental Stewardship

Setting the stage is more than preparation for the play. It is, in fact, the first dramatic act. In a sense, this chapter sets the stage for this treatise on stewardship. It introduces the reader to key concepts and begins to unpack what will become clearer throughout the book.

This book explores how the notion of stewardship shapes and is shaped by the practices of the church. Church practices are, of course, outrageously manifold and variable from place to place, but at the heart of the life of most parishes is the celebration of word and sacrament. It is a vain exercise to argue for the primacy of one or the other of these equally primordial activities. They form, as it were, bookends by which the church is defined. This exploration of stewardship begins with a treatment of the sacraments, and the last chapter treats the significance of proclamation for a theology of stewardship, while affirming that proclamation presumes sacramental activity, and vice versa.

We will begin this chapter by exploring the notion of sacramental stewardship as a *habitus,* or a way of being about the business of stewardship. We will next explore how baptism and Eucharist, in turn, engender in us a posture of awe and expectation, which sheds light on the task of stewardship to which all Christians are called. Finally, we will explore the relationship between awe and expectation, and consider the potency of these sacramental postures for the task of stewarding the gospel.

SACRAMENTAL STEWARDSHIP

To understand better the role of stewardship in relationship to the sacraments, it is important first to explore how the sacraments mirror the character of Jesus. Jesus has been called the primordial sacrament by some theologians, to underscore how he helps us understand baptism and Eucharist.[1] We begin, then, with the account of Jesus's encounter with the haemorrhaging women in Luke 8:42–48, which gives insight into his character and presence:

> As He went, the crowds pressed in on him. Now there was a woman who had been suffering from hemorrhages for twelve years; and though she had spent all she had on physicians, no one could cure her. She came up behind him and touched the fringe of his clothes, and immediately her hemorrhage stopped. Then Jesus asked, "Who touched me?" When all denied it, Peter said, "Master, the crowds surround you and press in on you." But Jesus said, "Someone touched me; for I noticed that power had gone out from me." When the woman saw that she could not remain hidden, she came trembling; and falling down before him, she declared in the presence of all the people why she had touched him, and how she had been immediately healed. He said to her, "Daughter, your faith has made you well; go in peace."[2]

1. Jüngel and Rahner, *Was ist ein Sakrament,* 36.

2. All Scriptural quotation are from the New Revised Standard Version of the Bible, except where noted.

It is interesting to note that in Mark's account of this same event, after the woman's clandestine encounter with Jesus's garment, Jesus asks, "Who touched my clothes?" (Mark 5:30). This changes in Luke, wherein Jesus asks, "Who touched me?" even though the narrative asserts that it is in fact the fringe of his garment that has been touched. This is extremely interesting, given that exegetes are often taught to see Luke (and Matthew) as correcting Marcan errors. Here Luke seems to introduce an enigmatic detail that problematizes our understanding of Jesus's presence. This problem is even clearer when Mark relates that the woman touches Jesus's cloak, while Luke relates that she touches "the fringe of his clothes." I can imagine describing someone as touching me if she has touched my shirt sleeve, but not if she has tapped the brim of my hat. What is the meaning of this?

This short narrative from Luke becomes for the church a parable that relates the expansive character of Jesus's presence. This story demonstrates that Jesus's self-identity exhibits a tendency to push the limits that would normally circumscribe his location. Of course, we are aware that this tendency is further seen in the identity of the church as the body of Christ.

There is an intentional ambiguity in this parable, as there is in the identity of the church as the body of Christ. The church is the body of the head, so a certain hierarchy is preserved that demonstrates that Jesus serves as master of his presence. Yet insofar as the parable deals with Christ's body, the identity of Christ stretches beyond what we first imagine. The consequence of this for the biblical theme of stewardship is that the mystery of the presence of God in Christ occurs under the rule of the sovereign Lord of heaven and earth, who deigns to call us as stewards of the mysteries (1 Cor 4:1).

The identification of the sacraments with the term "mysteries" is of a piece with the logic that God in Christ is present in, with, and under the sacramental activity of the Church. This presence is of a different sort than what we otherwise experience as presence, but it is a valid experience even in this difference. What is most important for this study is that we are called to be stewards of this presence.

The Greek word rendered as "steward" in the New Testament is *oikonomos*, described as "an official who controls the affairs of a large household."[3] This description has rightly been constitutive of most treatments of stewardship in parishes. What has too often been missing, in my estimation, is the fact that this treatment of stewardship—derived from an understanding of the economical practices of the early world—too often underestimates the manner in which stewardship is further defined by that to which it is rendered. It is one thing to be a steward of the material goods of a household, and another to be a steward of the education of a citizen in the making, but Paul's use of this word in reference to the mystery of the faith qualifies it still further. The notion of overseeing what is not your own holds true for those who are stewards of the mysteries, but stewardship is radically redefined by the idea that the presence of God in Christ via word and sacrament makes the steward capable of the assigned task. The ancient master chose stewards on the basis of demonstrated capacity. God turns incompetence

---

3. Wharton, "Stewards, Stewardship," 443.

into competence in stewards, precisely by granting them the task of stewardship. We do not rise to the occasion so much as we are raised to the occasion.

Stewardship in the church, then, is qualified by the recognition that stewards are birthed rather than made. God renders all Christians as stewards of the mysteries by virtue of their baptism, and some Christians as stewards of the mysteries by virtue of their ordination; in either event, stewards are crafted by God. Stewardship as it is understood in the New Testament is not a human possibility, but a divine actuality that enables a human response.

The practice of stewardship in the New Testament is further explained in Paul's admonition in 1 Cor 4:1, wherein he articulates his hope that Christians be regarded as servants of Christ and stewards of the mysteries. It is clear that Paul views the mystery as that revealed as the gospel (Rom 16:25). In content it includes the appearance of God in Christ (Col 2:2; 1 Tim 3:16), whose activities effect our inclusion in the life of Christ (Col 1:26–27), which means we shall not die, but shall be changed (1 Cor 15:51). The term "mystery" identifies God's mission. Surprisingly, it includes the hardening of the Jews, for a time, for the sake of inclusion of the Gentiles in God's all-embracing reign (Rom 11:25). It is the character of this mystery to be revealed by means of proclamation (1 Cor 2:1; Eph 6:19), which makes patent what was once latent (Eph 3:2–7). To this end, Paul describes himself as a minister of the stewardship of this mystery (Col 1:25–26).

The plural, "mysteries," occurs infrequently in the New Testament.[4] More common is the singular, "mystery,"

---

4. The plural occurs five times (Matt 13:11; Luke 8:10; 1 Cor 4:1, 13:2, 14:2), and the singular occurs 22 times.

which has a well-defined content throughout the corpus of the New Testament witness. Insofar as the majority of the New Testament allusions to the notion of mystery refer to it in the singular, what are we to make of Paul's one reference to us as stewards of the mysteries and the common tendency to explore this sacramentally?[5] Are the mysteries really the sacraments? If so, how do the mysteries of which we are stewards relate to the mystery proclaimed by Paul and those following him, according to the stewardship bestowed on all servants of the gospel?

In responding to these questions, we note that baptism and Eucharist are two of the three moments in the life of the church in which we first experience our own character as that of a steward. The third such moment is proclamation, which we will discuss in the last chapter of this book. We will consider first baptism and then the Eucharist, wherein we will come to see that sacramental stewardship is characterized by awe and expectation.

BAPTISM: TAKING TIME

Karl Barth, among others, was fond of speaking of salvation as an event. At the heart of his tendency to do this was his concern that it is too easy to make salvation an abstract concept. When this occurs, salvation becomes something of a notion, an idea, which Christians affirm by some sort of intellectual exercise. Alternately, salvation can be reduced to the maintenance of a well-ordered piety. In either case, the sovereignty of God is compromised, and

---

5. Senn's *A Stewardship of the Mysteries* is an important example of this usage.

the specter of the human as supposed master of his or her destiny raises its head.

Some see event language as the means of reclaiming the Reformation emphasis on salvation as that which happens to the Christian by the grace of God's election. Salvation, then, is something that happens. Moreover, salvation is a divine happening, as evidenced by the plurality of tenses used to describe it in the New Testament: we have been saved (Eph 2:8); we are being saved (1 Cor 1:18); we shall be saved (Rom 5:9). Salvation has not happened so much as it is happening. This is the nature of an eternal event. It simultaneously touches all of time. Baptism is such an event, and for this reason Luther, among others, encouraged a daily return to baptism.

Yet this emphasis on salvation as an event is more potent than it first appears, insofar as events happen in time and space. Humans tend to conceptualize salvation as otherworldly, with the result that a two-tiered universe constrains our religious imagination. Heavenly happenings take place outside of the constraints of time and space in which we live. This notion, of course, is completely undone by the narrative of God in Christ. Describing salvation as an event simply points to the manner in which salvation, like all events, requires both time and place. The sacraments point to God in Christ's promise to be present with the church in time and space.

It is, of course, true that both baptism and Eucharist are located in both time and space. Yet there is something about baptism that underscores the time character of salvation, and something about Eucharist that underscores the place character of salvation. Consequently, each sacrament informs the character of a sacramental stewardship in a particular way. Moreover, as I will show, baptism points to how sacramental stewards are astonished, and the Eucharist points to how sacramental stewards are expectant.

Baptism and Eucharist share many characteristics. Both were instituted by Christ, both convey the grace of God, both are received in faith, both are constitutive of the church in their material character, and both refer in various ways to Christianity's dependency on the narrative of Judaism. There are as many, if not more, differences between the two. Many of these are formal rather than material in nature. Yet there is one decisive difference between the two, and that is the question of repeatability.

Baptism is considered by nearly all of its proponents to be non-repeatable—a sacrament of initiation that is efficacious once and for all time.[6] This leads to the astounding claims associated with baptism as the means of inclusion in the life of Christ, wherein our understanding of time is reconfigured. Just as the biblical narrative deems the time preceding the coming of Christ as anticipating Christ, and all subsequent time as founded in Christ, so baptism is a sort of recapitulating moment. The time of Christ is considered kairotic,[7] in the sense that his is a time unlike any other. All of history finds its center point in Christ time, and in a related manner, baptism is the center point of our existence. Our time up to the time of baptism

---

6. Those who practice anabaptism do so only because they discount infant baptism as baptism proper.

7. *Kairos* is a Greek word used by theologians to refer to a revelatory moment in which time as we know it seems to be suspended. This is different from *chronos,* or ordinary time. The relationship between these two is further explored below.

anticipates it as the moment of our inclusion into Christ, in whom we were created "for good works, which God prepared beforehand to be our way of life" (Eph 2:10). Just as cosmic time is encapsulated in Christ time, all of our lives are encapsulated in baptism. The time of our baptism is eternal time—kairotic in character. Kairotic time, in opposition to chronic time, is what happens when eternity touches time. It is the primordial foundation of all time. This is why baptism cannot be repeated.

Baptism as non-repeatable and therefore kairotic engenders in its recipients a pattern of astonishment. Awe is simply the anthropological echo to the plenitude of the grace that is the communication of God in baptism. It describes how stewards live in time. Stewards are astonished because they realize that they are borne by the burden given them as stewards of the mysteries.

This is a constitutive feature of Christian life, and explains why Luther understood Christians' vocations to be given in baptism. At baptism, God calls each person to serve in the unique way appropriate to that person, for the good of the community. Taking up the cross that is appropriate to me is a baptismal task, because I am rendered a steward at baptism. Baptism is the beginning of my vocation as a steward, and because stewardship is baptismally founded, I can construe stewardship as a gift. I am free from the anxiety of ownership and the worry of loss, because I have nothing to lose save my identity as wholly construed by God in Christ, and I can lose that identity only by pretending to be someone I am not.

That this pretension pales in the face of grace is demonstrated in the fact that conversion back to Christ is not accompanied by rebaptism. The only opposite of the pretension of being self-made is a posture of astonishment. Astonishment is, consequently, a marker of stewards. Stewards are awed at the gift they have been given; they are astonished that the task itself gives them what they need to fulfill it, and equally important, they are awed by the plenitude of grace evident in the world.

Baptismal stewards see the world differently than pretentious directors. For those who live in the light of the kairotic moment, the world is thick with grace upon grace (John 1:16). When humans are stripped of the task of orchestrating meaning and feigning control, their resultant freedom is accompanied by the kairotic arrival of self-identity as sacramental stewards. In this moment, time itself is changed, and with the conversion of time, space itself is reconfigured.

We now consider how the Eucharist transforms space, and so makes stewards expectant.

EUCHARIST: TAKING SPACE

It is not the case that baptism alone reconfigures time and the Eucharist alone reconfigures space. In my estimation, however, each more clearly references one over the other. While the non-repeatability of baptism leads me to consider how baptism converts time, the parlance of presence suggests to me the importance of space as the primary referent of the Eucharist.

Even those Christians who argue most stridently against the real presence of Jesus in the meal finally enmesh themselves in arguments for real absence, which is as astounding a comment on the relationship of the Eucharist to space as is real presence. In either event, we construe the meal as the place wherein we locate Jesus. The meal finally asks the important question: "Where is Jesus?" No matter how the question is answered, it evokes the importance of thinking through the peculiar nature of this particular place, and of place in general.

It has long been argued that there is a difference between *chronos* and *kairos*—between the sort of time that marks calendars and the sort of time that births calendars, between the time of seasons and "a time such as this." But what is regularly forgotten is that God created us in such a fashion that we cannot think of time without thinking about space. This is evident in our frequent use of the term "timeline" to organize time spatially.

Space and time are not two separable entities that can be analyzed in isolated abstraction. The intersection of space and time suggests, in my estimation, that if there are two modes of time, then there are also two modes of space, which we might term "profane space" and "sacred space." There is space as we know it—the space of measurement, the space marking boundaries and inviting transgressions. This is profane space. It is the space of love and war, the space that charts our journeys from cradle to grave, the locus on the tombstone that names the places of both birth and death. We share such space with our fellow sojourners. But this is not the only space we inhabit. Sometimes, places are special—we could call them "sacred" as long as we do not fail to see that sacred and profane space are shared space, each overlapping the other. In fact, profane space already hints at its sacred potency, for those with eyes to see beyond the hurry that masks the profundity of our lives.

The rush that we script as our existence all too often precludes attention to what is astounding. I think this is especially true of the relationship between space and time. Every now and then, we get glimpses of the curious intersection that occurs between space and time. I unearth some fossil—literal or not—and realize that this place upon which I now stand has cradled a time before mine, and will cradle the time of those who will stumble upon this place when I am long gone. Space is hospitable to time; it welcomes all of time in its embrace. Every now and then, I realize that space is the most democratic *polis,* giving every time its say, and allowing every time that follows to speak its piece, as well. This realization that space can embrace time past, present, and future reminds me that space can also host the eternal. Such space is sacred.

The Eucharist makes a space sacred. It is for this reason that the ancients built altars on the relics of saints. They recognized that when eternity touches a space, it releases that space's potential; it makes of the space a place where all space finds its home. Just as past, present, and future coexist in eternity, all space takes its place at the sacred site. This is the logic behind the affirmation of the presence of the catholic body of Christ at the Eucharist. If the dead are in Christ and Christ is present at the Eucharist, then so are the dead in Christ.

All of this trades upon the realization that, in an important sense, sacred space is not like profane space. Profane space is competitive. If I stand here, then you cannot. Space needs to be negotiated between separate entities. But sacred space affirms that eternity makes possible the coexistence of separate entities. The risen Jesus shares space with the wood that is the door through which he walks. The scars of Jesus host the finger of doubting Thomas, just as the Eucharist hosts the no-longer-doubting Thomas. Our experience of sacred space transforms how we see all space, and indeed, how we experience time. Sacred space makes us expectant.

Stewards are expectant folk. We have encountered the risen Christ in bread and wine and, with the risen Christ, those who dwell in Christ by grace of his promise. But this promise, made to the saints at rest, is infectious, and it permeates us. We learn to live by promise, because promise characterizes us. Promise defines our character. We learn to live by promise, and we learn to make promises for the keeping.

Of course, stewards know that our promises can be made and kept only by the grace of God. An examination of promises throws us into an expectant state. We promise because we have been born anew by the promises of God, and so we are promising by nature. We are promising people—we live by promises and we make promises, and we do so by casting ourselves unreservedly upon the God who meets us in the resurrected one. We are expectant, because the new birth has caught us, has caught on. Stewards go to the table with gifts in train, expecting to meet the risen Lord, and leave the table expecting that by giving these gifts away, we finally and fully receive them. Sacred space engenders in us a posture of expectation. That posture informs our practice of stewardship.

In conclusion, we will consider the relationship between awe and expectation, and how they bear upon life in a church shaped by word and sacrament.

AWE AND EXPECTATION

At first glance, awe and expectation seem to be polar opposites. We are most often astonished by what we do not expect. When our expectations are met, "awe" is not the first word we use to describe the fulfillment we experience. It might be said that awe and expectation cannot coexist.

Yet, in the reign of God, things are not always as they first appear. Awe results from the new birth, and engenders in us a posture of openness. Those who are fully astonished will not turn in on themselves, but will open their eyes, hands, and hearts, precisely because that which has astonished them has taught them that love overflows. Love engenders love in an ever-expanding plenitude. We expect that love *will* grow, but we know not *how* it will grow, and we are ever in awe at the creativity of the self-communication of God in Christ. Stewards live by the promise that God will care for us, but we are ever astonished by how the divine promise is fulfilled. Consequently, we live in both awe and expectation.

For this reason, stewards live lives that are formed by both word and sacrament. It is easy to see the connection between stewardship and the word. The sermon is the time in the parish when we speak about stewardship. But it is given to the church to imagine how a theology of stewardship can also inform and be informed by a celebration of baptism and Eucharist in the life of the church.

Baptismal liturgies and eucharistic prayers that underscore the manner in which we are shaped by the sacraments into postures of awe and expectation could well serve a church with stewardship on its agenda. Insofar as these two church practices, along with proclamation, constitute the core of Christian existence, it is incumbent upon stewards of the gospel to imagine how a richer intersection between these key themes can enrich our lives together. It is delightful to be sacramental stewards, insofar as a posture of awe and expectation frames our way of being in the world.

In chapter 5, "Stewarding the Body," we will explore the relationship between ordained and lay stewards of the gospel, insofar as this very ordering makes possible our reception of the means of grace. As we continue to explore other aspects of sacramental stewardship in the chapters leading up to chapter 5, we will consider how a posture of awe and expectation informs our understanding of church practices. We will see how stewardship of the gospel shapes the multivalent character of church practice in such a way that the church's singularity of purpose is transparent: the church receives so it can give, and in giving, finally and fully receives the very gift it gives.

As we embark on this journey, we will first consider the limits of stewardship as a metaphor, as well as its relationship to justification. This point is of no small significance to Christians informed by Reformation insights. At the heart of that momentous time in the history of the western church was the realization that God's inversion of the human project in Jesus Christ is the foundational event of the re-creation of the world. This realization continues to characterize the church as being constantly reformed, and as a community of stewards shaped by the gospel—the gift that engenders awe and expectation in us.

2

Stewardship, Justification, and Justice

Luther described justification by grace through faith as the chief article of the Christian faith, on which the church stands or over which the church stumbles and falls. For Luther, "justification" refers to God's conversion of the human project. God in Christ enters human history, and we know that things will never be the same again. Even things as they were, in fact, are seen in a new light; the past is illumined by God's justifying act in Jesus Christ. God in Christ made new all of creation, as Paul so plainly declares in 2 Cor 5:17.

The Greek text is all-inclusive in its stark simplicity. Paul literally writes, "If anyone in Christ, creation new." The missing verbs allow us to read the sentence in two ways. On the one hand, we can read it to mean "If anyone is in Christ, he or she is a new creation." On the other hand, we can read it as "If anyone is in Christ, creation is new." Two different readings are legitimate, and each reflects truths to be found in the other.

We will now use these two interpretations of the sentence to point to related facts established by the act of God in Christ: God renders us just stewards, and God reserves the right to make right the world by rendering us stewards of justice.

JUST STEWARDS?

I introduce the theme of justification in this chapter to underscore the idea that God in Christ inverts the human project. We, who are by nature self-centered and prone to use others and the environment for our pet projects, have been put to death and made alive again. The new human is seen by God to reflect and bear the image of Christ, and is for that reason a recipient of the Holy Spirit, who renews us both from the inside out and from the outside in.

This work of God has the salutary effect of making us stewards in the reign of God. This much I have described and circumscribed in the first chapter. But at this point we need to ponder our identity as stewards who have been made just, and pose the question: "Are we just stewards?"

This question, too, reads in two directions. On one hand, "just" can be used as an adjective to describe how we are stewards who have been justified. On the other hand, "just" can serve as an adverb modifying the verb "to be": I am just/only a steward. Is this also true? To respond to this second question, a theological detour is in the offing— a detour offering insights into the relationship between stewardship and theology.

Students of the theology of the early church will be surprised to discover that the word "economy" frequently appeared in the parlance of the church fathers. It was most often paired with the word "theology," so the novice in the art of theology was given the task of relearning two words that had particular meanings when used together. For ancient church writers, "theology" referred to the being of God in God's very self (now more often referred to as "the immanent Trinity"). "Economy," most often translated from the Greek as "steward," referred to God's activity with respect to the world—that is, to God's creation, preservation, election, and redemption of those who had fallen. "Economy" included God's salvation of the world, which had been scarred by human sin and was groaning for a new beginning (Rom 8:22). Insofar as "economy" described the triune God—the Father who creates the world by the Word of the Son borne upon the breathing Spirit who saves fallen creatures—early theologians used the term "economic Trinity." "Economy," in short, referred to the actions of the triune God with respect to the creation, redemption, and sanctification of the world, while "theology" referred to God's very being as the Father who begets the Son, and through whom he breathes the Spirit, who in turn is the Love that unites them.

The interesting and even shocking thing about this is that our forebears in the faith identified God as one who works an economy—we might say they saw God as an economist.[1] "Economist," in this sense, is somewhat removed from the word as we use it in our workaday world, although not completely without points of connection. A modern economist examines and prods the workings of an economy, but does not manage that economy. This is a significant difference between a modern economist and an economist in the ancient world. An ancient economist or steward was very much involved in running the economy and affairs of the household, making it work as well as possible, fine-tuning it to derive maximum output from minimum input. The ancient economist had his fingers in

---

1. Meeks, *God the Economist*, 2.

the economy, tinkering to make it work as smoothly as possible.

Two points need to be underscored. First, recall from the last chapter that the Greek antecedent for "economist," which comes via Latin, is *oikonomos,* or "steward." In short, to speak of the economy of God is to refer to the stewardship of God. This, of course, is astounding insofar as God is more commonly rendered as the master, the owner of the household. And second, when God becomes a steward, the nature of stewardship itself and the identity of the steward him or herself is radically revisited, revised, and inverted.

All of this, of course, follows the logic of the incarnation itself, and the consequent identity of the Son as human. With this identity of the Christ as Jesus of Nazareth—complete with his life, death on the cross, resurrection, and ascension—humanity itself is transformed. Jesus perfects the human race by showing us what it means to be truly human. This identity of Jesus with the human—God become flesh—transforms human identity itself: to be truly human is to live in the life of God in Christ. In short, God in Christ changes what it means to be human, and as a corollary, God in Christ changes what it means to be a steward, and—if we dare follow where words lead us—he changes what it means to be an economist.

How, then, does God in Christ change this way of being, which is stewardship?

Martin Luther spoke eloquently of the redemption of humankind as the "blessed exchange." The blessed exchange is a theological explanation of 2 Cor 5:21: "For our sake he made him to be sin who knew no sin, so that in him we might become the righteousness of God." Luther explained the act of God in Christ as an exchange. God in Christ takes our place in becoming sin, but that is not the end of the story. By being in Christ, we who were sinners become ministers of reconciliation. The reconciler became sin so that sinners might be reconcilers.

This same logic directs the language of stewardship. In the ancient household, there were citizens, their sons, and their slaves.[2] The citizen owned the property and the slave. The son awaited his inheritance as patiently as he awaited his identity as a citizen. In a rough correspondence, then, the picture is one in which God in Christ becomes a steward for our sake. But this image, insofar as it mimics the logic of 2 Cor 5:21, also invites inversion: just as the Reconciler becomes sin so that sinners might become reconcilers, the Son becomes a steward so that stewards might become sons. Or, as Paul states in Gal 4:7, "So you are no longer a slave but a child, and if a child then also an heir, through God."

At this point, Scripture responds to a weakness inherent in the metaphor of stewardship: God's giving to us can be described in the language of lending only with some caution.[3] Most of the theology that treats stewardship rightly stresses God's identity as master and ours as stewards. We do not "own" anything that is in our "possession." All is given to us for our faithful exercise of stewardship. Yet Scripture also teaches that God renders us children of God; we are made sons and daughters of the most high in holy baptism.

---

2. Women in the ancient world were considered property, rather than persons. Their inclusion in the scheme of redemption, as in Gal 3:28, is for this reason astounding.

3. See Tanner, *Economy of Grace*, 47.

The stewardship model bends to the point of breaking here. One cannot simultaneously be a steward and a son; this is not an earthly possibility. It is, however, a divine possibility, by virtue of the fact that we who were stewards are made sons and daughters by the grace of the Son who becomes a steward. But our identity as children of God is an identity that is given us in Christ. In short, we who were stewards are made sons and daughter by being incorporated in (literally: put into the body of) Christ, who has become a steward. We, then, become stewards by first becoming children of God in Christ! This is our justification.

What does this mean? Are we just stewards?

Yes, in that we are stewards who are justified. No, in that we are not merely stewards—we are stewards who are simultaneously sons and daughters of God, because we are justified by the Father, who elects us as heirs in Christ by the power of the Holy Spirit. Just stewards are sons and daughters of the Father.

Our stewardship is given a particular tint by virtue of our identity as children of God. Just stewards attend to the well-being of the household of God, and of the world in which that household is located. We cannot be just stewards without caring for the people God has given us as neighbors, or for the world God has given us to tend.

We now consider what it means to be just stewards of justice.

STEWARDS OF JUSTICE

What is justice?

The church has a unique answer to this question: Jesus is our justice. This answer is not immediately transparent to outsiders, but it can be communicated in a meaningful way.

The Greek term for "justice" is *dikaiouse,* which is more commonly translated as "righteousness." The problem is that the church has tended to spiritualize this phrase, thereby losing one of the most important lessons learned from the chosen people. Righteousness and justice are about right relationships. Jesus is our justice because he demonstrates that a right relationship with God implies and entails a right relationship with our neighbors. At the heart of justice, then, is the maintenance of healthy relationships through honesty and forbearance. This is integral to the identity of the steward.

Earlier in this chapter I pointed out that "steward" is a translation of the Greek word that is also the antecedent of "economy." Stewardship and economy are not so far apart. Of course, we conceptually separate them in claiming stewardship to be something of a metaphor: we are and we are not stewards. We are stewards, because one day we will give up all we have. We are not stewards, because we are all children of the one heavenly Father, by the grace of his Son, who spirits us into and as a new creation.

The metaphor holds to a point, but metaphors always operate by means of both continuity and discontinuity. Our identity as sons and daughters of God represents the discontinuity, the point at which the metaphor breaks. What represents the continuity? What makes the metaphor of stewardship work?

Stewardship, Justification, and Justice

Stewardship works because we are spirit in body; we are spirited bodies in the world. To be human is to be in the world, in all of its glory and horror. Everything that makes the world what it is bears upon us, for both good and ill. In short, to be human is to be earthly. And nothing is quite so earthly as money, as we will see in the last chapter of this book. Money stands in for all we take from the earth and all we return to the earth. Money represents the give and take of human existence—and that very give and take describes the activity of the steward. To be a steward is to be engaged in the commerce of the household. To be a steward is to be engaged in economics, because money is the truck and trade of human activity. To be a steward is to attend to faithful and fair economic practice for the good of the household.

In the context of a modern economy, of course, good economic practice aims at a fair distribution of goods, or at least a fair and even opportunity to acquire goods. Contemporary economists would eschew such a vision of economy only to their own detriment, and politicians who deny such a vision in practice always espouse it in rhetoric. Of course, there are a variety of ways to locate that fair distribution. Social democrats believe the best society is one in which an equitable standard of living marks the body politic. Democratic capitalists aim for a society in which fairness means a level playing field. In either event, "fair" qualifies "good." Justice is marked by what is fair play for the good of the world.

The ancient steward worked for the good of the household. His aim was to order the household so as to create the conditions in which the good, the true, and the beautiful could flourish. The modern steward of public life aims for these same conditions, by creating an economy in which fairness itself flourishes. As we consider the theme of fairness as a marker of justice in stewardship, we find that the image of stewardship is an important tool in making sense of our commission to love justice, do kindness, and walk humbly with God (Mic 6:8). Yet this commission casts light upon the difficulty of being a steward: what is fair and just is not always easily determined or achieved.

Few people eschew justice. Even flagrant violators of justice will regularly point to the injustices they have suffered as reasons for their infractions of common law. It is given to judges, lawyers, and juries, in courts of law, to sort out what is just and how justice is best served. The work of such folk is reason for all to praise God, who has so ordered society that there is a mechanism to work for justice and equity for all.

Yet justice is a slippery concept, especially in its common guise as fairness.[4] Parents often lament the common echo of "It's not fair!" in family life. The lament reflects the fact that determining what is fair can be skewed by both the finitude of our ability to perceive what is fair and our inability to apprehend justice, insofar as we await the day

---

4. Aristotle notes the *sui generis* (kind unto itself) character of justice in his treatment of virtues in *The Nicomachean Ethics*. Most of the virtues he discusses can be considered in terms of two ditches into which the ethicist can err. The virtue of bravery, for instance, can be seen as a mean between cowardice and foolhardiness. Generosity can be seen as a mean between profligacy and stinginess. Justice, however, cannot be defined as a mean in the same manner. There is either justice or injustice, which is the negation of justice. There is something different about justice, which Aristotle considers the chief virtue.

when we will finally know what is really fair. Justice is, finally, an eschatological category.

Both of these factors—the finitude of our ability to perceive fairness and its eschatological character—demand further exploration. Consider first the manner in which finitude limits our ability to apprehend what is fair.

I remember one of my parishioners telling me of a battle between his six- and four-year-old daughters. After carefully cutting a remaining piece of cake in two, the father gave both girls a piece of cake. The youngest was insistent that her piece was smaller, and demanded justice. The father wisely took the two plates into the kitchen, out of sight of the two girls, and cut one piece in two. Upon receiving the plate with two pieces in place of one, the four year old was delighted because she now had two pieces of cake. Of course, the other option would have been for the father to invoke the "whoever doesn't cut the cake gets the first choice" rule. But here, too, fairness can be slippery. If I am to cut, fairness will depend on my ability to cut well, and if I am four and my sister is six, she will be able to take advantage of my inability. Perhaps the six-year-old ought to cut the cake and the four-year-old get first choice. But even here, problems can ensue. Remember, this is the same four-year-old who thought she had more cake when it was cut into two pieces!

This silly example is also serious. This is especially clear to those who have negotiated inheritance battles. A certain heirloom can bear more symbolic weight than it would ever merit in financial recompense. How do you balance the value of Grandpa's well-worn Bible against that of the sofa in the corner? What is fair? If what is fair could be easily determined, the wisdom of Solomon would not be in such high demand.

Beyond the difficulty in determining what is fair, justice is made further opaque by the fact that sometimes it takes time to determine the worth of a thing. We have all read newspaper tales of children selling inherited paintings that have been collecting dust in cellars and eventually found to be worth hundreds of thousands of dollars. The values of things are not absolute. If fairness is about value, and value is a moving target, at what time do we mark what is fair? And who decides this? There is a flighty quality to the fair and the just.

This is no reason to despair of doing justice. Justice and its correlate fairness are most often manifestly apparent. It is simply wrong when women and men are paid differently for the same work. It is unfair when qualified applicants get passed over for certain jobs because they are immigrants. Justice can usually be apprehended and acquired in increasing degree. This is the business of the body politic, and the church is as surely a citizen of this reign as any legitimate organization that exists for social good and the betterment of citizens.

Significant lessons can be learned as the church works for justice in various struggles. One of the most poignant lessons arises from the truth-and-reconciliation work in South Africa.[5] Charles Taylor, in reflecting on this work, has noted that this experiment in hope has taught us that wrongs are not always made right by money. A strong sense of justice and injustice can sometimes engender hatred in the hearts of those who perceive a wrong. Taylor notes that this is precisely what necessitates the wisdom to balance both the contextual factors that determine the good

---

5. See Taylor, *A Secular Age*, 698–706.

in a given circumstance and the reality that more than one good in a situation might demand attention. Resolution of the quandary of justice requires enhancing relationships for the betterment of life together.[6] This does not mean economic matters are irrelevant, but while money can stand in for the goods that I deliver, it can never stand in for the good that I am. And I can stand with you only in the proximity afforded by the transparency of mutually vulnerable relationships, not by coerced relationships. There is neither truth nor reconciliation when one party has nothing to lose.

What does this mean for life in the parish?

STEWARDSHIP, JUSTIFICATION, AND JUSTICE

The Augsburg Confession of the Evangelical Lutheran Church affirms that the church is the assembly of believers among whom the gospel is purely preached and the sacraments rightly administered.[7] How is justice related to this? Is doing justice an appendix to the event of justification, as experienced in word and sacrament?

Many Christians want to affirm the significance and indispensability of doing justice, but become squeamish at the thought that our justification is in some way dependent on our doing justice. That would be the undoing of the gospel, the happy news that God in Christ makes us right apart from and in spite of both our angry refusal to do what is good and our inability to will well in the state of sin. Protestant Christians have always prided themselves on the affirmation that we are not saved by good works.

6. Taylor, *A Secular Age*, 705–6.
7. "The Augsburg Confession," in *The Book of Concord*, 43.

Of course, this is a half-truth. Clearly, we are not saved by our good works, but surely we are saved by God's good work. This is the sometimes forgotten bit of the message of justification.

We too readily say we are saved by our faith, instead of by God's work, all the while subtly making faith our very own work. But the good news is that faith is God's working in us. The accent is ever on God. More important, word and sacrament engender in us a posture wherein we look for the working of God both inside and outside the church. Evangelical Christians look for the good working of God righting any situation wherein relationships are compromised. It is our duty to name the work of God wherever God in Christ fulfills the Magnificat by the power of the Spirit. It is our delight to join in! God works through us and awakens us to the reality of the divine undoing of the power of sin. This must be at the heart of parish life: we are to name the justifying work of God and join in justice by working for right relationships. But how does this translate into life together?

First, a disclaimer: failure is not only allowed in a gospel community, it is expected. The good news is that failure is the means whereby God in Christ meets the human in his or her most vulnerable condition. To achieve justice, we must do something!

For most parishes, this begins with getting to know the community—an increasingly difficult and important step. In a culture driven by cars, it is a valuable exercise (in more ways than one) to walk around your neighborhood. Pastors and lay people alike ought to knock on the doors of their neighbors. Get to know where you are: visit local drop-in centers, shop locally, attend community events.

These are all part and parcel of striving for justice; you cannot achieve justice merely by writing a check. The gospel message is that justice is accomplished by meeting, befriending, and being with people. This, of course, is one of the most troubling trials of modern discipleship. We live in a culture that believes we can do everything, and so we most often do nothing.

Striving for justice means deciding what *not* to do, as well as what *to* do. But one thing is sure: when justice is understood as being about relationships, the justification of the sinner is the event wherein God accomplishes justice by word and sacrament, allowing us to participate in divine fullness. The justified *truly* live abundant lives as disciples of Jesus, who is the truth.

But the pressing question we ponder, as stewards of the gospel, is how we are to live with money, that enigmatic currency of Caesar. We turn now to this.

3

Stewardship and Fundraising

IT IS NO SMALL irony that much of the recent valuable, well-meaning work with respect to stewardship has resulted in less talk about money. The need to talk about stewardship in a broad sense has sometimes resulted in stewardship programs that skirt around the issue of currency. It seems that time and talent have eclipsed treasure.

In this chapter we will look more carefully at the phenomenon of money, exploring what happens when what we say about gospel truths foundational to our life in the church touches treasure. How do we view money through the lens of the gospel?

We will first look more carefully at money as a symbol, considering both the power and ambiguity that attend currency. We will then consider the place of fundraising in communities that live in Christ. We will use key Reformation learnings to ponder what a spirituality of fundraising might look like. In particular, we will consider the so-called Reformation *solae* ("alones") themes of grace, Christ, cross,[1] Scripture, and faith in relationship to the sometimes mundane task of fundraising.

---

1. See Luther, *D. Martin Luthers Werke: Kritische Gesamtausgabe,* 5.176. "The cross alone is our theology" is the translation of Luther's original "*CRUX sola est nostra Theologia.*" The emphasis is Luther's.

POWER AND AMBIGUITY: TOWARD A THEOLOGY OF MONEY

How are we to speak of money in the church? We must consider the ambiguous reception of money as a symbol in our culture before considering its circulation in service of the gospel.

The well-known verse "The love of money is the root of all kinds of evil" (1 Tim 6:10) and Jesus's admonition that we cannot serve both God and wealth (Luke 16:13) point to the particular temptations attending money.

Money's greatest strength is its ability to wear many masks. It serves as a stand-in for labor, work, and wisdom, as well as for their products. This is what gives money its flexibility.

Attending that flexibility, however, is a sort of ambiguity, most frequently voiced in the aphorism "There is no clean money." The truth of this statement is reflected in the fact that the object we hold in our hands has passed through many hands, some of which have used it for services beyond the pale of morality. To hold money, in this sense, is to hold the human condition in all its glory and horror.

It is impossible to abstract money from this gut-level recognition of its symbolic power. Money is, in a sense, a chameleon. In one instance it appears in an exchange between drug lords, and in the next it is used to admit a patron to hear Bach's *St. Matthew Passion*. What happens when this same bill enters the church and finds its way onto the offering plate? Has it found its resting place? Of course not! Money not only travels to the church, it travels through the church, meriting its nickname, "currency," which is rooted in the Middle English word *curraunt,* "to circulate." Money itself shows that the distinction between the sacred and profane is forever blurred. For this reason, many perceive money as a necessary evil.

But such an assessment is impossible for stewards of the gospel, who recognize that our certitude about the distinction between sacred and profane more often serves our own interests than God's. What we determine to be outside of God's reign (profane) might not be so in God's sight. What we determine to be profane might simply be the sacred on its way.

Stewards of the gospel, then, are agents through whom God works to redeem money, so as to make of it a contagion of salvation. In the world, only illness is considered a contagion. In the reign of God, health itself is contagious. Whatever God touches is made whole, including money—a topic of great interest for our Lord. Part of this task involves speaking clearly about both the potentials and the dangers of money.

The steward is the servant who understands that only by using time, talent, and treasure together, under the lordship of the Spirit, can one escape the potential idolatry of money, and in so doing turn it into an icon of the sanctification of the profane by the sacred.

STEWARDSHIP AND THE SPIRITUALITY OF FUNDRAISING

Using "fundraising" to describe the sharing of treasure within the church might be deemed counterintuitive. "Fundraising" is an increasingly forbidden phrase in church circles, conjuring up images of desperate devices, dodgy raffles, and embarrassing means to get money into the coffers, apart from the necessary act of opening our wallets and giving away hard-earned money. Fundraising is heard as a thoroughly profane phrase, but I want to reclaim this word, believing there is a certain profundity in the profane.

In the first instance, we want to remember that "fund" itself comes from the Latin word *fundus,* which means "ground" (or "foundation"). Fundraising, then, is about raising the ground, and so invites us to imagine fundraisers as those involved in one of the most audacious of all tasks.

In the second instance, the spirituality of fundraising is about the gospel's mandate to "equip the saints for the work of ministry," and so invites fundraisers to be faithful stewards of the task given them. This presupposes that God has given to certain folk the task of raising funds. To fail to engage in this task is to miss out on the delight of exercising a spiritual gift given by God. The task of raising funds is the means by which God calls others to give of themselves by giving money to a particular work within his reign. In this manner, fundraising enables others to exercise the spiritual gift of giving. Both the giver and the asker are fundraisers—the former by raising funds, the latter by creating opportunities to give.

All of this presupposes an understanding of spiritual giftedness that is first construed communally. More often, however, we see a spiritual gift as the exercise of an individual for the sake of a community. This view is deemed commonsensical, and properly so, for it demonstrates what happens in the exercise of a spiritual gift. But such a perspective needs further exploration.

While it is true that I serve the community with my gifts, it is also true that I am served by that community. Individual efforts within the reign of God are utterly dependent upon the communal conditions that make it possible for me to engage my gospel gifts. Just as my writing depends upon the writers I have read (and often interiorized, by the grace of delight and provocation), so, too, are our very actions enabled by the communal activities that have made us who we are. When I exercise a spiritual gift, I not only engage what the Spirit has given me, I am also engaged by those the Spirit has given me. I act with the community that has brought me into existence and that sustains me.

The place of fundraising in the church, then, is about the Spirit's calling individuals within the church by way of the church within the individuals. I am the gift I am because others have given of themselves to me. Fundraising is a thoroughly communal reality. I give because others have given, and because I give, others in turn can give. There is a delight in this—and beyond the delight there is a duty to invite others into this delight. Stewards share the gift of giving. Fundraising is about community.

We will now explore a theology of fundraising by examining it through the Reformation *solae:* grace, Christ, cross, Scripture, and faith alone. Each of these theological touchstones will inform our understanding of the spirituality of fundraising.

Grace Alone: Fundraising Ordered by Grace Is First Fund-Seeing

Theology informed by the Reformation assertion that we are saved by grace alone through faith alone for Christ's sake takes as its point of departure the thoroughly dependent nature of human life with God, which is to say of human life in totality. We are utterly dependent upon God—saved by grace. The church's proclamation of this truth is consistent and continuous. Sunday after Sunday, we eat at this table. Day by day, we drink from this font. In its insistence on the habit of regularly hearing the good news, the church can articulate a decidedly countercultural perspective on the nature of life.

The culture around us is obsessed with novelty. Things are assessed under the canon of novelty. The value of what I use is conditional upon its contemporaneity. This cultural presupposition is most evident in our fixation with the utility of technology, although it is also manifest in other cultural fixtures, such as design and fashion. It is hard to imagine it could ever have been different. Yet it surely has been. Stasis, rather than evolution, was the goal of cultures for millennia before the mania of change that has marked modern history. Our unfamiliarity with the potency of the familiar itself is hardly surprising. Yet exactly the power of the habit of hearing the gospel is at the heart of a life of awe and expectation. The surprise of grace is built upon the gospel's familiarity. The gospel is what it is by virtue of its continuity: its proclamation of the risen Lord.

The habit of hearing the gospel produces a familiarity that breeds conviction and compassion, rather than contempt. This familiarity does not gainsay an element of novelty in the exploration of this gift of grace that ever gives. But in this other kind of novelty, this authentic novelty, what is truly new is a richer knowing of what I already know, rather than a replacement of one thing by another that's altogether different.[2] In other words, the arresting quality of the proclamation of grace lies in the realization that I do not altogether know what I already know. Grace invites me to ponder what is at hand—it reins in my tendency to run from this to that in a mad obsession with what is next and new. Grace awakens me to the gift of life.

Lest you feel lost in hopeless abstraction, consider the following manner in which Annie Dillard illustrates the awakening that is grace:

> Knowing you are alive is feeling the planet buck under you, rear, kick, and try to throw you; you hang onto the ring. It is riding the planet like a log downstream, whooping. Or conversely, you step aside from the dreaming fast loud routine and feel time as a stillness about you, and hear the silent air asking in so thin a voice, Have you noticed yet that you will die? Do you remember, remember, remember?[3]

Dillard invites us to consider that the one we call Lord is the author of time and eternity. Our immersion into awareness of time is an awakening of the sense of the eternal in us, and precisely in this awakening grace, we begin to see through the lens of our march from cradle to grave. At its best, this awakening alerts us to the astonishing realization that we are, rather than that we are not. At its worst, this awakening grasps our very hearts with an anxiety that paralyzes us and makes our passage through time merely formal. But when grace serves as the pedagogue of

---

2. Jorgenson, "Authenticating Novelty," 191.
3. Dillard, *An American Childhood*, 151.

our awakening, we are ushered into a posture of awe and expectation. As the apostle reminds us (2 Cor 5:17), "So if anyone is in Christ, there is a new creation: everything old has passed away; see, everything has become new!"

This newness is of the sort that reclaims the curiosity of youth for all. Our passage through life is too easily a devolution from inquisitiveness to critical distance. In childhood, we lean forward to see more closely what engages us. In time we are taught to be skeptical, critical, and hesitant. We no longer lean closer for a better look, but step back to look from a distance. That which interests those obsessed with dignity invokes in them a distanced posture of disinterested mastery.[4] This is the antithesis of grace. Grace awakens in us the vision of wonder and the realization that yeast yields loaves. Grace announces that things are not always as they seem.

Those who have been awakened by grace are given new eyes to see. The first response to the event of our salvation, as we saw in the first chapter, is a posture of awe, or astonishment. This astonishment, however, is not amorphous. The "wonder of it all" is focused on the giver of it all—God in Christ. In Christ we have been conditioned to expect God to meet our need, and in Christ we have that need met. The awe of it all is that Christ is ever meeting us, and our experience of salvation is one in which our need is ever being fulfilled.

Salvation, then, is a reorientation of our eyes. We see in a new way, because we see in *the* way: we see from Christ's perspective. Our vantage point is the richness of God. Those who see with Christ see potency where oth-

---

4. Dillard, *An American Childhood*, 109.

ers see deficit. They see richness where others see poverty. Moreover, they see that those who are literally rich are theologically poor save through the gift of giving. Fundraisers are first fund-seers, because they see the foundation that is Christ, and they see that the *fundus* upon which they build is none other than Christ.

Christ Alone: Fundraising Informed by Christ Is Political

It is interesting to note how the word "politics" is used to characterize certain activities as suspicious. That which is "political" is by definition suspect.

Things have not always been so. Among others, the Greeks and Romans understood the construction of the *polis* ("city") to be a noble and necessary human endeavor. In fact, politics has been considered a virtuous activity for the better part of human history, and examples to the contrary merely demonstrate why it is so important that statecraft be done well.

Of course, we know this to be true, and our degradation of an otherwise noble word simply demonstrates our confusion around how best to do what we know needs to be done. Politics, at its simplest, is the arrangement of community for the sake of a project or projects that benefit humanity. Fundraising is, for the reason, political.

Seeing fundraising as political is the very reason many eschew it. Behind this propensity to label it as profane, however, is a view of the church that fails to take seriously the lessons learned in Christology.

The early church struggled hard to discern how it could properly be said that Jesus is both human and divine. For many in the early church, the former became most problematic. Early theologians variously pictured Jesus in a way that protected his divinity from his humanity. Some did so by imagining his humanity as phenomenal, rather than real; some did so by suggesting that only certain parts of Jesus, such as his soul, were actually divine, and the other parts were mundane; yet others did so by suggesting that Christ's humanity and divinity never tainted one another by way of a union.

The church responded by asserting that Jesus was fully human and fully divine, and that a proper Christology necessarily reflected this. This assertion is significant insofar as it underscores that God in Christ embraces the mundane. Not only was Jesus fully human, he was—precisely because of his humanity—socially located and invested in the culture in which he lived. God's pattern of salvation, initiated in the concrete community of Israel and culminating in the Jew named Jesus, embraces rather than excludes humanity in its fullest expression. For this reason, the reign of God does not exclude politics and its attention to the commonwealth of the people.

The implications for fundraising are significant, particularly with respect to our sometime discomfort around the means by which community functions. Community functions well by way of connection. Politics works by way of establishing and maintaining points of connection between parties. "The body politic" refers to the organic means by which communities function.

This is as true for the church as for the community of Christ. The image of the body—as one of the most significant ways to reference the church—reflects the fact that politics are part and parcel of life in the church.

This is also true for fundraising. Yet this does not make fundraising more spiritual or less spiritual than any other activity within the church. Fundraising is as dependent as every other exercise of the gifts of the Spirit in its realization. Just as preaching depends on administration within the context of church life, so fundraising depends on teaching, healing, and so on. The interdependence of all the gifts given the body of Christ also applies to fundraising. This fact can correct the misunderstanding that fundraising is a profane task, preparatory to the sacred activity of preaching. Fundraising as informed by Christ reminds us that all parts of the body are needful, and therefore holy. Those who raise funds invite all of the body to participate in life together—a truly gospel task.

Cross Alone: Fundraising Under the Cross Lays Bare Power

Money is power.

This truism displays both the range and the limit of the relationship between money and power. Money is power, yet we cannot say that power is money. Money is circumscribed by and parasitic upon power. Money functions only by grant of the legal tender upon which it trades. Money's power, then, is derived from the authority given it by community consent. Jesus demonstrated this with his enigmatic referral to the question of the temple tax.

Currency functions under the aegis of those in authority. Its decision to use money indicates the church's entanglement in the world, although one might suggest that the world is first entangled in God's decision to grant authority within the world. Scripture narrates the creation of power and its abuse, but also its reclamation under the gospel. In sum, Scripture narrates creation, redemption, and the relationship between the two.

But what is the relationship of creation and redemption with respect to stewardship? To answer this question, a theological detour on the subject of creation and fall is in the offing.

The doctrine of creation introduces us to the question of authority. God established the world according to the biblical narrative, with lines of authority and the power consequent upon them. Yet the narrative of the fall points to the recurring abuse of power. How, then, ought we to understand authority and power, in light of their identification as created gifts, albeit gifts corrupted by vices founded in the fall?

This is a singular instance of a more general question: how are we to understand created gifts after the fall? One response to this question emerges in the period of the late Reformation, shortly after Luther's death, in the Lutheran communion. The question came in the form of a question concerning will.

Human will, of course, is a gift of creation. After the fall, the Lutherans considered free will to be fallen, and therefore bound in our propensity to sin. This was especially problematic for some, who identified will in some fashion with God's image, in which humans were created. This raised the question of whether free will constitutes the image of God.

This question was more difficult to answer, yet it was necessary to answer it, since the nascent Lutheran community, with Luther, wished to affirm that free will could be attributed to God alone.[5] Following Luther, the will that operates freely does so only insofar as the divine will moves in and with it. The human under sin, then, is clearly out of relationship with God.

Does this mean the human has no will? The early Lutherans said no, clearly asserting that the will existed, yet not freely. Some suggested that this meant the image of God was not only lost in the fallen human, but thoroughly obliterated. Yet this solution was not finally embraced. Many felt it was going too far to interpret the fallen will as the obliteration of the image of God. Such an interpretation would suggest that it would be possible to be human without God, or alternately, that those who were not saved would not really be human. In the final analysis, the fallen will is seen as dependent upon God, even in its fallen state.

The lesson is that fallen creation anticipates and is ordered toward redemption, even in its deviation from its purpose. This is of a piece with Luther's treatment of law and gospel.[6] Law is simply God's modus operandi in anticipation of gospel. The upshot is that authority and power, even in their fallen conditions, anticipate their own redemption. They cannot be seen as pure evil, or they

---

5. Luther considered "free will" an attribute proper to God alone, since being truly free is a possibility only for the One who orders all things. Human "freedom" is at best conditioned, and at worst a fiction. See Luther, "On the Bondage of the Will (1525)."

6. In Lutheran parlance, "law" refers to God's demands of us, while "gospel" refers to God's promises to us, kept even when we fail to do our part. This distinction is critical, as is Luther's differentiation of the first use of the law (the order implicit in creation) from the second use of the law (the demand placed upon the creature after sin). See Jorgenson, "On the Art of Distinguishing Law from Law."

would be nothing but a lack, insofar as everything that exists is good (Gen 1:1–31). Evil is like a disease that exists only by its dependence on what truly is.

But that is hardly the biblical construal of authority and power. The human is given dominion as caretaker. Authority and power are tools for taking care of creation. To exercise this dominion is the vocation of the human, although it must be affirmed that authority in the reign of God differs from what is commonly experienced in the world. Gospel authority is kenotic in nature. The economy of reversal that marks the Gospels sketches the contours of gospel authority. Just as the greatest are the least, so those with the most authority are most willing to share it. Divestment is the path to plenitude in the reign of God, so gospel authority and power are exercised in a countercultural fashion.

We see this within and outside of the church. It is given to us to consider our response to this gift.

Scripture Alone: Fundraising and the Narrated Gospel

Some years ago, narrative budgets became popular within stewardship programs. Narrative budgets endeavor to tell how money is spent for church missions. There is a curious tendency in our culture to understand questions of finance as a kind unto themselves. It should be self-evident that money is part of a community's story, yet we tend to divorce questions of finance from those of mission. Annual church meetings often have a sort of schismatic agenda, insofar as reports of church life are often dealt with apart from the budget review. Yet the budget is part of each report, and each report is part of the budget.

This is certainly the way things operate in Scripture.

Jesus spoke often of money, but always in the context of mission. Jesus locates all of the parables and teachings about money within the trajectory of his mission as God's redeeming love in the world. Money is not external to God's mission, but integral to it. This is not too surprising when we consider the money re-presents who we are. Money functions as a kind of placeholder that allows us to participate in God's mission.

Consider the following story from Henri Nouwen's *The Spirituality of Fund-Raising*:

> During my own fund-raising work, people have said to me: "I will give you money if you will take up the challenge to be a better pastor, if you will stop being so busy and more faithful to your vocation. You run around and talk your head off, but you don't write enough. I know that this is difficult for you—to shut the door and sit behind your desk and not speak to anyone—but I hope that my contribution will support you in your writing." This is part of the fruitfulness of the community of love.[7]

This story illustrates that when we ask folk for money for our mission in the world, we invite them to participate in it. We invite them into the story we tell. At a fundamental level, fundraising is nothing less than providing a person with the opportunity to add his or her voice to ours in proclamation of the gospel. Proclamation is a symphonic event, bringing together a community of voices and roles. It functions best when each plays his or her part in harmony. Inviting people to contribute to our cause is properly

---

7. Nouwen, *The Spirituality of Fund-Raising*, 31.

understood as asking them to champion and participate in it. They are truly present with us, even in their absence.

This presence in absence is probably one of the least understood truths of fundraising. People give to causes that matter to them because they are personally invested in these causes. Although the money they have given is no longer theirs, in a sense it continues to *be* them. That is why the abuse of donations is so earth-shattering. If I give to a cause that I believe to be valuable and important, and it turns out to be a sham, I suffer from this discovery. It pains me to know this money has been wasted. But how has it been wasted? One could argue that it really hasn't been wasted, because it is no longer mine. But I don't experience it that way. In my heart of hearts, I know a difference, and the difference is that I have been personally compromised. Trust has been broken, and broken trust affects me at a personal level.

Faith Alone: Fundraising Is How Faith Communicates

The grace of God creates receptive hearts that ache to speak of the gift they have been given.

This desire to communicate is integral to the life of faith, and communication is manifold in its forms. We not only say something with our words, we also say something with our actions. And we say something with our money.

Money is a communicative tool. Our use of money is the means by which we present ourselves in the world. Frugality, constraint, moderation, liberality, and extravagance are not just how we spend our money, they are how we *are*. Language betrays the truth of this. When we say Frank is frugal, we don't just say Frank uses his money frugally. Frugal is how Frank *is* in the world. Money is an indispensable tool for being in the world. Whether we have little or lots, what we do with it tells people how we are.

This is of astounding importance for fundraising. People don't give money just to help a cause; they give money as a way of being in the world, as a way of saying who they are.

Some years ago, the seminary where I work was facing a significant financial challenge. Our office received a letter from an elderly woman who said she was saddened to know we were facing severe financial constraints. She was further saddened by the fact that she only had five dollars to send, but she sent it anyway. That five-dollar bill was her way of saying who she was. She shared herself with that bill. This was among the most moving letters we received, and it gave us confidence for our future. It reminded us that our supporters were accompanying us in our trials.

It also reminded us that money is one way we give ourselves to others. It is not something external to our being. As a communicative tool, money bears our being and represents us in the world. People arrive in church and in the world via their use of money. Money is not external to people, but a fixture of their being.

What consequence does this have for fundraising?

Here we return to our initial insight. The grace of God in Christ creates in us a posture of awe and expectation. Yet there is more to this. We who have been touched by grace find in ourselves a propensity to act in accord with the One who has acted with and for us. We have a desire to mirror, as far as possible, the kenotic character of love. This desire grows wholly out of our desire to be like the source of our redemption. This is a perennially frustrated desire. We always fail to measure up to the One who saves us. Yet God in Christ does not demand this of us; God calls us to be whomever he has saved us to be. There is a freedom in this, for which we should give thanks.

We need to reclaim a biblical notion of thanksgiving. For humans today, the word "thanks" can be so perfunctory that it is meaningless. Thanksgiving in Scripture was not something said, so much as something done. The Eucharist is the paradigmatic event of thanksgiving. At the Eucharist, in response to the gift given at the altar, we orient the whole of our lives to the mystery that is not resolved, but further deepened by immersion into Christ, the primordial and final *mysterion.* Fundraising is a means by which stewards of the gospel give thanks for the inexhaustible richness that constitutes our lives.

As we have noted, fundraising is etymologically descended, in part, from the Latin word for "ground." Is it possible to raise the ground? At first blush, fundraising seems as impossible as that. Yet theologically, fundraising must be understood as a divine rather than a human possibility. This truth does not exclude our engagement in the activity of fundraising, but it locates the power and the possibility of this activity in God's promises. God is the guarantor for the activity; it is God who raises the ground, though we are used instrumentally to do so.

Like so many things in the reign of God, instrumentality is understood differently than we might first imagine. God does not use us without thereby making us agents of the reign. God not only works through us, God also works in such a way that we work, too. Discovering that this is our end makes our participation in fundraising more than a means to another end. Fundraising is part and parcel of our God-given task of proclaiming the gospel so that all may know God raises the ground in divine delight.

Such a realization forces us to our knees—yet we are not speechless, because stewards of the gospel pray.

We will now consider what it means to be a praying steward of the gospel.

4

The Praying Steward

AT AN INTUITIVE LEVEL, prayer and stewardship seem to be natural if not necessary partners. Stewardship programs most often frequent parishes facing financial crises. Crisis seems to be the fuel that most often flames prayer. The connection seems commonsensical.

But significant problems arise when we begin from this point. Why should financial woe be the primary point of commonality between stewardship and prayer? Is crisis the only—or even adequate—fuel for prayer? What would a stewardship of prayer look like?

It is these questions that hazard our venture into probing the praying steward, and a hazard it is. To enter the theme of prayer is to be immersed in a mystery so near to human identity that it can alter how I see myself and the God who has spoken me into being so that I might speak. Awe and expectation beckon.

The theme of prayer as it emerges in Scripture is framed by two limits: the command to pray always and the command concerning how to pray, as unfolded in the Lord's Prayer. We will begin with the former and then attend to the latter.

PRAY ALWAYS

Paul commands us to pray always (1 Thess 5:17). When I have broached the topic of prayer in adult membership classes, we have most often discussed this passage at length. It points to the impossibility of prayer.

This is a good beginning point for speaking about prayer. Prayer is not a task like others. To pray always is to recognize two fundamental truths: first, prayer is a means of communication, and second, prayer is a gift and then a task.

We will begin with the second of these truths.

Prayer is initially a gift and subsequently a task. This points us to the first lesson we learned in Prayer 101: to pray is to speak. But speaking itself is no small feat. In fact, prayer is a captivation by the mystery of language itself. One of those small but significant wonders that once fell upon me as I led a bible study on Genesis was the realization that the creation narrative does not record the creation of language. Language is not a creation of God, but a gift of God's own self. And while we cannot and must not say communication is God, we can and must say God is communication.[1] This reminds us that our speech betrays our finitude, yet points to traces of God's image within us, bearing us about as we enter the vocation of being human, which has at its heart the august task of communication.

When we think of speech, what comes to mind is the lecture at the podium, the converse over the fence, and the table banter that makes of life a joy. But beyond these, we realize that a more fundamental talk takes place: inter-

---

1. "In the beginning was the Word, and the Word was with God, and the Word was God" (John 1:1).

course with God. This is primordial speech. It is an echo of the fact that God has spoken us into being.[2] We speak because we have first been spoken. Our speech moves, then, in two directions: we speak to one another and we speak to God.

Adequately addressing either of these topics is beyond my ability, yet insofar as I find myself practising both, it is incumbent upon me to reflect theologically on what they mean. Here I will restrict my reflections to what it means that I address the God who has addressed me.

I once had a bishop who, in speaking of prayer, made the simple observation that a life of prayer begins with the belief that prayer works. If we try too hard to discern the intricacies of how it works, we will be hopelessly shackled. There is some wisdom in such a starting point. I also remember speaking with a friend who did not pray, because the idea of prayer was so rife with enigmas that he found it impossible to practice or commend. There is less wisdom in this. Indeed, if I were to follow this logic of refusal, I would quit speaking with Homo sapiens, as well as with the master of heaven and earth! The foundation of prayer, as we shall soon discuss, is rooted in the divine command, rather than in my ability to sort out the enigmas of communication.

Communication truly is mysterious and enigmatic. Yet this drives us deeper into the subject. We must look at what it means to communicate with God, paying special attention to the most prominent enigmas.

---

2. Gen 1:1—2:4a narrates the creation of the world, including humans, by the divine Word.

Opponents of prayer most often attack a childish notion of prayer that purports to unmask the pretension that our supplications change God. The stock response, of course, is that prayer does not change God, it changes us. Yet, the opponents complain, if God knows what we need, why not just give it to us? Why bother with the give and take of asking and answering? Again, we reply that a relational view of prayer points to the gift of intercourse. At the heart of prayer is the delight and the mystery of two who share of themselves. God calls us out of ourselves and into life in God, precisely by encouraging prayer from the one who ventures the risk of relationship with the triune God.

Yet at the heart of this risk is a truth more fundamental and demanding. We read in Rom 8:26–27:

> Likewise the Spirit helps us in our weakness; for we do not know how to pray as we ought, but that very Spirit intercedes with sighs too deep for words. And God, who searches the heart, knows what is the mind of the Spirit, because the Spirit intercedes for the saints according to the will of God.

Here we are introduced to one of the most curious characteristics of prayer. There is a kind of prayer that is God praying within me. My understanding of prayer at this point is utterly at ruins; this kind of prayer is the Spirit interceding in us, for us, to God.

Is this not a monologue? How is this to be intercourse?

Stewardship reminds us that all that we are is a gift of God. This includes our speech—*all* of our speech. We speak only because God has spoken us into being and now speaks in us. But is this truly communication?

This important question trades upon an understanding of genuine communication as occurring only between two self-sufficient agents of equal stature. If this truly qualifies real communication, then no, prayer is not communication. But we can think differently about communication. Communication, as we will further explore in the last chapter, is best understood first as self-communication, a giving of the self so the other might *be*. This simply articulates what parents, among others, already know. Intercourse begets and bears fruit who are in the first instance the self-giving of the parents, children who first speak because they have been spoken to. Words do not come instinctively. They must first be given to one who has been given life. Speech itself is a gift, as the aforementioned passage from Romans 8 demonstrates.

Yet this passage deepens our apprehension of the truth that language is truly a gift as understood theologically. Not only are we *first* spoken to so we can speak, we are also *continually* spoken *to* and *through* so we can speak. What Paul describes is an existential condition. This is what it means to be a human. The Spirit ever speaks through me, because weakness is not a once-in-a-while condition; it is the way I am. I am weak and utterly dependent on God. This describes what it means to be a steward. Not only are my time, talent, and treasure a gift from God, so is my tongue. I cannot speak without first being spoken to and spoken through. In this occurrence I am indeed free to speak, and speak I must. In fact, the Apostle tells us in 1 Thess 5:17 to pray always.

What does this mean for the steward of the gospel?

I have described prayer as a means of communication. Communication takes place in various ways. I speak to my family face to face and on the phone. I send letters, e-mails, and faxes to friends and others. Communication takes up the better part of my life. In fact, I think one could quite cogently make the case that communication takes up all of my life—communication is what I make with my life.

I tell something to everyone round me by what I do with my life. My choice to live in this section of town rather than that, my choice of car (or to forgo a car altogether), what I do with my leisure time and my hard-earned dollars, how I relate to my family—all of these decisions say something to the world about what I value, and what I value says something about who I am.

But this is not yet enough. More important is the fact that all of my decisions say something to God.

In a sense, Paul's imperative to "Pray always!" can be read as an indicative: "You are always praying." We do pray constantly. We are ever saying something to God. We speak to God of our valuation of the environment by what we do with it. We speak to God of our estimation of others by how we engage them. We speak to God of how we receive the gift we are by how we use our time, talents, treasures, and tongues in the world. Paul's admonition to pray always alerts us to the fact that we say something with our lives. We announce our self-identity as stewards—or not—by how we walk upon this earth. Do we wander about as masters who live without any sense of accountability? Or do we walk aware that every breath is a gift, every sight a revelation, every encounter an awakening? To be aware that we pray always is to live *intentionally*.

This truth, of course, can be received as either law or gospel. For most of us, law has the louder voice. For this reason, Paul's admonition to pray always prepares us to receive Jesus's prayer into our hearts, where a pattern for prayer is formed under the aegis of grace.

PRAY, THEN, LIKE THIS

The Lord's Prayer is really one of the most astounding of gifts given the people of God. It astonishes us by its breadth of comprehension, and engenders in us a posture of expectation by schooling us to pray for what we might not dream to be within the realm of possibility.

In what follows I will simply ponder each petition, paying special attention to what it means for a steward to pray this prayer. But first, a short comment on how this prayer fits into the pattern of the gospel is in order.

This prayer is called the Lord's Prayer because Jesus teaches it to us. Of equal importance is the fact that this prayer is commanded. Martin Luther makes mention of this. At first blush, Luther's invocation of the command aspect of prayer makes it appear to be wholly law. But as he continues to explore what it means to pray this prayer, a new tenor attends my hearing:

> Furthermore, we should be encouraged and drawn to pray because, in addition to this commandment and promise, God takes the initiative and puts into our mouths the very words and approach we are to use. In this way we see how deeply concerned he is about our needs, and we should never doubt that such prayer pleases him and will assuredly be heard.[3]

3. Luther, "The Large Catechism," 443.

The Lord's Prayer is an astonishing gift, because it frees me from the question of whether I pray aright. Too often, our experience of communication includes manipulative agendas, hidden prejudices, and inability to listen. These patterns are easily transposed into our communication with God. The Lord's Prayer, however, comes to us from Jesus's mouth. These are *his* words, given to us so we can pray to the Father. This prayer announces God's agenda and initiates God's will for the world. At the heart of the story of salvation is the wonder of the Word become flesh in Jesus of Nazareth. This is a bold, resounding shout from the highest mount to the entire world. The Lord's Prayer is that very same message in the guise of an echo.

In a sense, the Lord's Prayer has a relationship to Christ that mirrors that of word and sacrament, in which Christ gives us the words we need to carry out the divine will. When these very words issue from our mouths, we participate in a divine action. We pray the hallowing of God's sacred name, in which we are baptized. We pray the coming of God's reign, which inverts structures of injustice and betrayal. We pray the doing of God's will, and in fact do God's will in so praying. This is a divine moment in the life of the collective church and the individual Christian, and the Lord's Prayer is given to us to tend, steward, and use in service of the coming reign. We are stewards of this prayer.

I will now comment on the seven petitions, as found in the Matt 6:9–13, to clarify what it means to be a steward of the Lord's Prayer.[4]

4. I offer my own translation of the Greek text here. I do this not to commend yet another version for use, but to highlight some themes lost in the two translations most often used liturgically in North America.

Our Father, Who Is in the Heavens,
Hallowed Be Your Name[5]

Matthew's Gospel variously uses the terms "heaven" and "heavens." The use of the plural undoubtedly reflects his Jewish interests. "Heavens" is a more faithful translation of the Hebrew word for "heaven," which is in a plural form. It is intriguing that Matthew doesn't always use the plural, and that, in fact, the Lord's Prayer has both the singular and plural. It seems fitting to highlight the use of the plural in this instance.

Other significant usages of the plural occur in the repeated phrase "reign of heavens." Matthew often—but not always—changes Mark's "reign of God" to "reign of heavens." Matthew's other significant use of "heavens" is found in the opening of the heavens in the baptismal narrative (Matt 3:16). While Mark seems to use "heaven" to name a place, he seems to use "heavens" to reference the divine self. The splitting of the heavens in the baptismal narrative suggests a rupture of God, whereby God makes patent the divine will for the world.

It is important that the Father referenced at the beginning of the Lord's Prayer is the Father in the *heavens*. The allusion to the baptismal narrative and the reign sayings is of decisive importance. The name to be hallowed, sanctified, and made whole is the name of the One who sent Jesus to be baptized and who sends the Spirit. This

---

You will find these translations in *Evangelical Lutheran Worship*, 112. In the rest of this chapter, I will place the petitions from these two versions into footnotes, for comparison with my own translations. The traditional rendition will be followed by the more contemporary.

5. Our Father, who art in heaven, hallowed be thy name/Our Father in heaven, hallowed be your name.

is the One who works the inversions enunciated in the reign-of-God sayings.

The key point is that God is at work. The heavens have been opened so God is *seen* to be at work. To be a steward is to have this action as your point of reference. God exposes the divine self as the Spirit tumbles from the heavens to rest upon the Son sent in God's mission. God is at work in the sanctification of the divine name.

In bidding this petition, the believer prays for completion of the first table of the law, in which idolatry and the misuse of God's name are prohibited and keeping of the Sabbath is commanded. This petition reminds us that we need God's name to be hallowed, because the baptized live in that name. The wholeness of God's name is the condition for our wholeness.

In the first petition, we seek a saving place from which to pray:

Your Reign Come[6]

The reign of the heavens is the inversion of life as we know it.

The Magnificat (Luke 1:46–55) first intimates that God's modus operandi in Jesus will be radical. Jesus's own parables of the divine reign confirm this. They announce that things are not as they first seem. God's reign is like a mustard seed, that smallest of seeds that grows great to host the birds of the air (Matt 13:32). This reign is likened to the hidden and mysterious leavening of bread (Matt 13:33). The heavenly reign is like laboring in a vineyard with a profligate owner (Matt 20:1–16). It is a marriage

---

6. Thy kingdom come/Your kingdom come.

feast in which slaves gather in all, but from which the king chooses few (Matt 22:1–14).

There is something unwieldy in these descriptions of this coming reign. The reign of God does not often accord with my sensibilities. It is often assaulting. It unsettles my propensity to presume that God's reign ought to accord with my sensibilities. To pray the coming of the reign of God is to invite chaos. This is what we do every time these words sneak out of our mouths without our realizing what we have let loose. We invoke chaos without knowing it! It is no wonder that we cannot make sense of life. We pray for senselessness, and God answers our prayers, because the reign of God trades in the stuff of disorder—but disorder of a peculiar sort. This is disorder only when viewed from the perspective of earth.

Stewards of the gospel have another vantage point. With one eye looking up and one eye looking out, we pray:

Your Will Be Done, as in Heaven, so on Earth[7]

We begin again by attending to "heaven." In this instance, we find this important Matthean noun in the singular. Matthew often uses the singular "heaven" in tandem with "earth" (Matt 5:18, 18:18, 28:18). He also uses it to describe the place of birds and angels (Matt 6:26, 8:20, 13:32, 22:30, 28:2). He describes heaven as the footstool of God (Matt 5:34). Jesus looks up to heaven when he prays (Matt 14:19).

---

7. Thy will be done on earth, as it is in heaven/Your will be done on earth, as in heaven.

"Heaven" references a place above, which symbolizes where God is. Its pride of place in the petition "Your will be done, as in heaven, so on earth" is therefore important.

Heaven points to eternity. Earth points to time.[8] Heaven hosts the realized will of God. Heaven is that eternal place and time that consummates all places and times. In heaven, the reign of God finds its rest; inversion is no longer needed. Yet the doing of the will of God in the interim occurs via eternity's incursion into time. When eternity enters time, the earth is wrested from its comfort and bent hard to meet heaven. For the will of God to be done, justice cannot be ignored; sin cannot be countenanced; truth unearths the lie that deviously buries the first table (prohibition against idolatry, the misuse of God's name, and the commandment to keep the Sabbath) and therefore the second table (all the other commandments).

God's will, however, is the attainment of the commandments in the lives of his people. In the Lord's Prayer, we boldly bid its realization for us.[9]

It is no accident that Matthew places this prayer within earshot of the Beatitudes, which eloquently identify what a citizen of heaven looks like. To pray the Lord's Prayer is to evoke the content of the Beatitudes: poverty of spirit, a mournful yearning for justice, a merciful heart that aches for peace, and a willingness to suffer the persecution that signals a time reined in by eternity.

This suffering love knows that eternity tackles one day at a time, and so we pray this day:

---

8. See Aquinas, *Catechetical Instructions*, 166: "God is stated to be in 'heaven' in that he exceeds corporeal things."

9. Luther, "The Small Catechism," 357.

Give Us Our Daily Bread Today[10]

Of the seven petitions, this one most immediately calls to mind stewardship themes, especially in light of the many bread images in Scripture. Our bread comes to all people from God, day by day. The children of Israel teach us that hoarding it stinks. God gives enough for all, but by way of the give and take that makes relationships. Bread is a foundational sign in Scripture. Aquinas suggested that this petition serves to counter human propensity for greed, ingratitude, anxiety, theft, and gluttony.[11] This is indeed a tall order for six succinct words.

Luther makes an important addition to the ecclesial conversation about praying for our daily bread. His Small Catechism tells us that bread in this context is a stand-in for all that is required to meet our needs.[12] His Large Catechism takes the petition deeper into Christian life. Following this line of thought, we realize that there is no bread without baker, yeast, and flour. And flour, for instance, comes to us by the contributions of farmer, field, sun, and agrarian tools. But the field, to cite one more example, might not be productive save for the prince who keeps marauders at bay. In sum, everything is connected, and to pray for bread is to pray for all of the stars to align so the loaf might make it to my table. Our Father in the heavens is concerned about earthly life, and this most material of all the petitions reminds us that even the so-called profane comes to us from God's hands.

---

10. Give us this day our daily bread/Give us today our daily bread.
11. Aquinas, *Catechetical Instructions*, 181–86.
12. Luther, "The Small Catechism," 357.

But this is not all. The fourth petition tells us *how* to pray the Lord's Prayer. It commands it as a daily prayer. The Lord allows us to pray only for today's bread. Tomorrow's bread is not on today's agenda. We will need to pray this prayer tomorrow. This fourth petition drives this prayer into the day to day, that most mundane of time. The give and take of the work-a-day world is the stage set for the divine drama wherein the Father's name is hallowed, God's reign comes, and we plead that God work the divine will:

And Forgive Us Our Transgressions, as We Also Forgive Our Transgressors[13]

We do well to remember that this petition does not lead the prayer. Recall the content of the first four petitions, remembering that as we make each petition, God answers it, day by day. Simone Weil notes that the prayer for God's reign implies our forgiving our debtors.[14] As we pray for God's name to be hallowed, God's reign to come, and God's will to be done—and as God answers these prayers—we forgive others, because that is the content of the will, reign, and hallowing of God's name.

Weil notes that our prayer for the reign of God unlooses our claim on the future that has seeded bitterness deep in our souls: we realize that our grudges are grounded in our affront over the fact that our transgressors have spoiled the futures we have so carefully orchestrated. As the heavens' reign overshadows us (Matt 17:1–13), we allow ourselves to receive the future as a gift from God. The

---

13. And forgive us our trespasses, as we forgive those who trespass against us/Forgive us our sins, as we forgive those who sin against us.

14. Weil, *Waiting for God*, 224.

condition for forgiveness is fulfilled in the hallowing of the divine name, the coming of the reign, and the doing of the divine will.

But what if I haven't forgiven my transgressors? What if I can't?

Aquinas notes that the "we," "our," and "us" of the petition reminds us that this is the prayer of the church, and can for that reason be prayed by someone who is still at enmity with a debtor.[15] This observation places this petition within the practices of the church. As a communion of saints, we confess our identity as a community of sinners. Confession and forgiveness take place in the rough and tumble of life together. Forgiveness—both my being forgiven and my forgiving—is an eternal process that begins in baptism and ends at the end of time, and which is mysteriously present to us in the sacrament of the altar. We live between these two eternal moments in the church. Our forgiveness is not contingent on doing what is not ours to do, but on God's doing in us what God alone can do. We forgive our transgressors because God works the divine will in us.

This same will emboldens us to pray:

And Lead Us Not into Trial[16]

While serving as a pastor, I had a parishioner who was bothered by this petition, telling me he really preferred the "save us from the time of trial" version.

I must admit that this conversation cemented my discomfort with the modern translation of the sixth petition

---

15. Aquinas, *Catechetical Instructions*, 192.
16. And lead us not into temptation/Save us from the time of trial.

of the Lord's Prayer. I am rather nervous about a translation that resolves a problem that is not so easily dispensed with in the Greek version. Moreover, the translation seems to harbor the (I assume) unintended reading of "save" as Jesus's teaching us to pray so God might *rescue* us from the time of trial—a thoroughly sensible prayer, but decidedly not the one given in this petition. "Save," as in *spare* us from the time of trial, is marginally truer to the text, although the most problematic element of the petition remains too easily solved. In Greek, we clearly read, "Lead us not into trial." In Greek, the negative particle immediately follows the "and," in fact, and so begins the petition. To do justice to the text, we have to admit that Jesus teaches us to ask that God *not lead* us into trial. Why this way of praying?

In the first instance, the petition as it stands in Greek reminds us that God very well could lead us into trial. This is not impossible. No a priori definition of God precludes such an action. The master of heaven and earth is not subject to our definitions of God. Such a God would not be sovereign.

Yet we need to consider the verb that has been lost in the modern translation. The older version uses "lead" to describe what God does. The new version uses "save." Of course God does both, but the next petition describes the *saving* God. This petition describes the *leading* God—the God who is with us, in front of us, forging the way, with saints and sinners in train. We lose this picture of God as Immanuel at our peril.

Finally, it is important to remember who teaches us to make this petition: Jesus. Jesus does not teach us to pray for something God has no intention of granting. In short, God's response to this prayer is "I will not lead you into trial or temptation."[17] Because we pray this prayer daily, we are existentially confronted with the realization that God in Christ has elected *not* to lead us into trial. Knowing that Jesus teaches us to pray in this manner reminds us that God will not lead us into trial or into temptation, because the Father answers affirmatively the prayers crafted by Jesus. So we concur with Luther:

> It is true that God tempts no one, but we ask in this prayer that God would preserve and keep us, so that the devil, the world, and our flesh may not deceive us or mislead us into false belief, despair, and other great shame and vice, and that, although we may be attacked by them, we may finally prevail and gain the victory.[18]

Luther's explanation of the commandment points us in a helpful direction. The language of victory presumes our participation in a battle of some sort (see Eph 5:10–17). Luther believes that in the battle with sin, death, and the devil, God remains at my side, so I live. God will never withdraw; for God to withdraw is my destruction. Luther does, however, envision the possibility that I might withdraw from God's side and fall into evil. And so we who have need of the leading God also need the saving God, a truth of which we are reminded in our practice of daily confession.

For this reason, we pray:

---

17. The Greek word *peirasmon* can be translated as either "trial" or "temptation"; the context determines the definition. I contend that "trial" is the stronger meaning intended in this petition.

18. Luther, "The Small Catechism," 358.

But Deliver Us from Evil[19]

Aquinas suggests that God answers this petition in four ways.[20] First, God preserves us from the affliction that we name "evil." This, in Aquinas's estimation, is a rare occurrence. Second, God delivers us by consoling us in the midst of evil. Third, God delivers us from evil by so blessing us that we forget the evil that might otherwise absorb us. And fourth, we see in the evil that has afflicted us a pedagogical function that mitigates its affliction.

These solutions variously satisfy us in making sense of the evils in which we find ourselves implicated. At least they address the fact that we find ourselves beset by evil. The Lord's Prayer, then, ends with a stark realism: sin, death, and the devil continue to afflict us as we await the hallowing of God's name, the coming of the divine reign, and the realization of God's will.

Luther's explanation of this petition points to the eschatological character implied in this last petition:

> We ask in this prayer, as in a summary, that our Father in heaven may deliver us from all kinds of evil—affecting body or soul, property or reputation—and at last, when our final hour comes, may grant us a blessed end and take us by grace from this valley of tears to himself in heaven.[21]

We pray for a blessed end. "End," of course, refers to both purpose and completion. To pray for a blessed end is to pray for a reason to live well and for a life well lived.

---

19. But deliver us from evil/And deliver us from evil.
20. Aquinas, *Catechetical Instructions*, 198, 199.
21. Luther, "The Small Catechism," 358.

In either event, we need a good guide to navigate our journey from cradle to grave. We who have had to do with tour guides know of two sorts. On the one hand, most of us have had the tour-bus experience, where the guide delivers the same lines over and over, pointing out interesting facts. There is some—albeit limited—utility in this sort of guide. But there is another sort of guide. From time to time I join a tour guide at an art gallery or museum. This is an altogether different sort of guide. These guides are infectious in their passion for their subject matter. They interact with patrons; they ask and invite probing questions; they teach us how to see. They guide us in the discipline of expecting the unexpected. They fill us with awe. This is the sort of guide the Lord's Prayer is. It is an interior guide, because the Lord of the Lord's Prayer lives within us.

Evil is not easy to explain, and the Lord's Prayer does not try. Yet the Lord's Prayer can be a guide in making sense of the evil we face, helping us identify our Father in the heavens as the One who saves us from evil.

Stewards of prayer learn to pray with two eyes. One eye is ever attentive to the way God in Christ works wonders that leave us in awe; the other eye is on the lookout for what God is up to in the world, the church, and the individual. Prayer is therefore properly at the heart of stewardship. We can pray only because God has suffered death in Jesus, in order that we might be drawn into resurrection life, a life that frees us to speak with God. This gift gives the community of faith a way of life that renders us humble and hopeful.

This vocation of prayer—this giving of ourselves to God by sharing our deepest worries, our greatest joys in thanksgiving, and our most profound thoughts—is one of the most significant means by which we realize ourselves and make ourselves available for the work of God's reign. Through prayer as a means of faith, God's grace transforms body, church, and world.

These last are the concern of the next chapter, as we continue to ponder what it means to be stewards of the gospel.

5

Stewarding the Body

WHAT DOES IT MEAN to steward the body? What does "body" refer to?

These questions invite us to consider the significance of the body for the task of the steward, who approaches all in a posture of awe and expectation.

We will first explore the stewardship of the body proper, as the locus for our self-identity, then consider the stewardship of the body of Christ and of the world as the body writ large. We will conclude by examining how the body proper, the body of Christ, and the world exist as three indivisible realities that hinge one upon the other.

STEWARDING THE BODY GIVEN

St. Paul, in writing to the community of Christians at Rome, begins the latter section of his letter by speaking of fundamental practical matters. Note well how he begins this portion of his epistle:

> I appeal to you, therefore, brothers and sisters, by the mercies of God, to present your bodies as a living sacrifice, holy and acceptable to God, which is your spiritual worship. Do not be conformed to this world,[1] but be transformed by the renewing

1. The phrase "this world" is actually "this age" in Greek.

of your minds, so that you may discern what is the will of God—what is good and acceptable and perfect. (Rom 12:1–2)

This passage is important for two reasons. First, it presumes that the body matters. Christians sometimes act as if the body were nothing more than a carriage carrying the soul about. Paul does not seem to hold this opinion. Second, this passage demonstrates that as the body is involved in worshipping God, it is transformed by a renewing of the mind. This observation alerts us to the fact that Paul understands the body and mind to be of a piece.

Paul's interest in the body has too often been forgotten in the church. From time to time, however, a theologian alerts us again to the importance of the body.

Karl Rahner, one of the most significant Roman Catholic theologians of the twentieth century, wrote an important book entitled *Spirit in the World*.[2] This astounding book is evocative in many ways, but most important, its very title invites the steward to consider what it means to exist bodily.

Rahner's dissertation is not about the Holy Spirit, which one might expect at first blush. Rather, this is a theological anthropology. Rahner describes what it means to be human, first defining human as "spirit in the world." Rahner does not imagine the human as some free-floating, disembodied spirit; for Rahner, and for many other theologians, embodiment is at the heart of human identity. Yet he describes the human as spirit in the world because he understands that our first experience of the world *is* our bodies.

2. See the bibliography.

Sometimes we imagine the self as absolutely distinct from the world. This is, however, a thoroughly mistaken notion of what and who we are. The human is spirit in the world because our bodies are utterly and thoroughly worldly. We are constructed of the stuff of the world—our materiality admits the sort of examination that can be exercised on other worldly objects. Like rocks, our bodies can be analyzed for iron and other constituent parts; like trees, we can be measured to determine our dimensions; like all parts of the world, our bodies can be broken into pieces. Yet we are more than our bodies. We are also individual spirits. Poetics as much as physics define our existence. Rocks do not cry, nor heal others rocks with tales that recite their genesis. Humans are both spirit and world. The church recognizes the marriage of world and spirit as constituting both our glory and our burden. The human is located within the world. To be embodied is to be worldly. But *are* we bodies, or do we *have* bodies?

It is commonsensical for us to talk about having bodies; at one level we do "have bodies." Our bodies are subject to our control, which is why we can talk of stewardship of the body. Those who are stewards exercise management over something given them. This is also true of the body, because our embodiment involves more than bodies. Sheer materiality does not define our existence, and our ability to be more than we are defines the self-transcendence that is the glory of being human. The condition for the possibility of stewardship of the body is its objectification: I master who I am only by self-differentiation, by seeing that I can be someone other than who I am. Most often, in some fashion or other, this self-mastery includes mastering my materiality.

This is hardly rocket science, but the correlate point that demands a hearing is not so easily received.

We not only have bodies, we are bodies. Human existence is not parasitic on the body. My body does not just "host" me; I *am* my body. Memory, thought, and volition exist only by grace of the sensory information my body provides. This way of understanding humanness differentiates Christian thought from platonic thought. For the ancients informed by platonic ideas, the essence of the person was the immaterial soul, which yearned for release from the body. By contrast, the early church asserted the necessity of bodily resurrection in asserting life everlasting. The resurrection of the body, not the immortality of the soul, was at the heart of an Easter faith. Moreover, this understanding of existence emphasized the significance of corporeality for all modes of human knowing, faith included. Sacraments are so readily embraced because they satisfy our thirst for knowing via our senses.

We not only have bodies, we are bodies, and these two themes point to particular qualities of the task of the stewardship of the body. That we *have* bodies speaks to our ability to master the body for the sake of the reign of God. That we *are* bodies speaks to the fact of our bodily existence. The task of stewarding our bodies is itself a gift. Stewards' exercise of managing materiality includes self-management. That we can do so points both to our capacity for the self-transcendence of poetics and to our transcending selves, which revel in the pure gift of physicality. All humans, however, are surely frustrated in our experience of both self-transcendence and our transcending selves. Because we are bodies, as well as have bodies, we experience our bodies not only as the means by which our transcendent selves achieves self-transcendence, but also as the means by which we experience the world as inflexible, demanding, and immobile.

Our experience of our bodies is as ambiguous as our experience of the world. Scripture narrates our engagement of both world and body in a remarkably parallel fashion. On one hand, Scripture points to the shadowy side of both. The cares of the world, like the lure of wealth, distract the Christian (Mark 14:19). The world did not know Jesus (John 10:1). The world hates Jesus (John 7:7), as it does the believer (John 15:19). Neither Jesus nor the disciples belong to the world (John 17:16), and the world does not know the Father (John 17:25). The wisdom of the world is foolishness with God (1 Cor 3:19), and saints will judge the world (1 Cor 6:2). The affairs of the world distract the believer (1 Cor 7:33). In fact, friendship with the world is enmity with God (Jas 4:4). In like manner, the body is described as that from which we need rescue (Rom 7:24), and is considered dead because of sin (Rom 8:10). The old self was crucified so the body of sin might be destroyed (Rom 6:6). The circumcision of Christ puts off the body of the flesh (Col 2:11). The body is what needs to be kept in check (Jas 3:2).

This strand of thought about the body, and more generally the world, replicates the sometimes extreme pessimism that Plato and his heirs exhibit toward the material. Matter participates in being at a lower level in platonic thought, and the philosopher aims to attain a certain disinterest toward the body. The body is to be pummeled for the sake of the mind. Something of this is seen in some strands of New Testament treatment of the body and the world. Yet this is not the final word about world and body.

The New Testament also exhibits astoundingly positive assessments of both—and oftentimes in the same books. We read, for instance, that the body is the temple of the Holy Spirit (1 Cor 6:16–20). In so describing the Christian, Paul replicates John's description of Jesus's body as "temple" (John 2:21). Matthew (6:25) and Luke (12:23) both describe the body as more than clothing, thereby suggesting that the body is more than a mere dwelling place for spirit. Paul, in fact, suggests that the body has the august task of bearing the death of Jesus (2 Cor 4:10).

The body can be both bane and blessing, because the body, like the world, admits the possibility of transformation (Phil 3:21; John 3:17). Jesus is described as Savior of the world (John 4:42), whose flesh is the life of the world (John 6:51). The disciples are sent into the world so the world may believe (John 17:18, 21). The world is the recipient of riches and reconciliation as a result of the rejection of Israel, with the consequence that the acceptance of Israel will result in superfluous blessings (Rom 11:12–15). This strand of thinking reflects the Jewish inheritance that constitutes the church. Because creation is good, all that is created is good, and this is what we are called to steward.

Because our first experience of the world is our experience of our bodies, our task of stewarding the body is already an instance of stewarding the world. To steward the body, then, is to face creation in both its horror and its glory—in both the wrenching dangers of a fallen creation and the ecstatic experiences of plenitude and giftedness. To be a steward is to face the ambiguity of the body and the world, an ambiguity scripted into the Bible. When God commands the primal pair to exercise dominion over the world, that exercise begins with the body, wherein the world is first encountered. Stewarding the body is first stewarding that bit of the world circumscribing the self. The body provides the steward with an opportunity to craft the practice of stewardship. It presents a bit of creation within our control, which manifests both the agony and the glory of the created order. This microcreation is given to us as stewards to tame, temper, empower, and utilize for the glory of God.

We must remember that the body is stewarded toward an end. This end is dual in nature: it is the church and the world. We turn first to the former.

STEWARDING THE BODY OF CHRIST

The biblical affirmation of our corporeality is most clearly seen in Paul's willingness to use "body of Christ" as a reference for the church. But as we move from a discussion of stewarding the body as individual to the notion of stewarding the body as corporate, we face two related and difficult issues.

First, we need to specify in some meaningful fashion exactly what we are called to steward when we steward the body of Christ. Second, we need to contemplate who holds responsibility for this exercise of stewardship. When we speak of our stewarding the body of Christ, are we usurping Christ's headship? If not, will our understanding be a top-down or a bottom-up notion of stewardship? Will we look for the church to be modeled after the fashion of a democratic *polis,* or as a benevolent dictatorship?

First to the question of what is to be stewarded—the body of Christ. When I ponder my experience of stewarding my body, I can readily identify the responsibility due this corporal and intellectual existence, and the emotions that result when the two meet. I can locate something of a core in my agency, wherein my being in the mode of intellect and body meet. In sum, I steward my thoughtful actions. Can the same be said of the body writ large? Can we locate a centre in the body of Christ, a mode of being wherein it can be said that the church *is* this? If I, as an individual body, am my actions, then what of the corporate body? Does the corporate body, which is the church, act as a body?

These questions have classically been answered by considering the nature and mission of the church.

Of course, it is affirmed, the church acts as a body. It is clearly asserted by many that the church's actions have a center, in that it celebrates word and sacrament. These activities define the church. They are both singular and manifold: there is an activity in the church called preaching, yet this activity is expansive in character. There is preaching in the narrow sense, and there is preaching in the broad sense. The same is true of the sacramental life of the church. Both word and sacrament are the means by which the church bears witness to the presence of Christ and thereby communicates his presence to hearers. In the narrow sense, word and sacrament speak of the presence of Jesus to the gathered community. In the broad sense, word and sacrament are writ large as the ethic of the church. Christians live out their experience of word and sacrament by using their activity in the world to reiterate what they have heard inside the church. If I am what I do, and the same can be said of the church community, then this community is word and sacrament. To steward the body of Christ is to steward word and sacrament—the points of discussion of the first and last chapter of this book.

Stewarding the Body

But can anyone really be identified as steward of the body of Christ? If I am steward of my body, would not Christ be steward of his own body?

The problem with this latter, conditional question is that it presumes Christ receives his body in the same fashion I do. This is exactly what cannot be affirmed. I receive my body as pure gift, which makes me steward of my body, because my body belongs to God. Christ, however, does not receive his body (either as his local presence or as the church) the way I do mine. In Christ, the Logos becomes flesh. The incarnation narrates the kenotic[3] decision of the Logos. Christ is not a steward of his body in the same sense I am, because a steward, by definition, receives what is given for him or her to tend. Christ is not first steward of his body, but Lord of it. This cannot be said of us. Indeed, we who are stewards deign to be lords, while the true Lord hands over his body to stewards! As Lord, Christ kenotically calls forth stewards to tend his body. But whom does Christ call to such stewardship? Is the church as a whole called to be steward of the body it constitutes, or are certain people, such as ordained ministers, stewards of the body of Christ?

Paul's appeal to the image of the body in his epistles, together with his insistence on the varying gifts marking the baptized, anticipates the important question asked by many Christians: why should this one rather than that one preach, teach, baptize, and celebrate?

This is a good question, and should not be answered too hastily. After all, the logic of the imagery of the body

3. The word "kenotic" comes from the Greek word for "to empty." Its most famous usage is found in Phil 2:5–11, in which Christ's incarnation is described as a self-emptying for the sake of all.

of Christ assumes that stewardship of the mystery is a task given the body as a whole. It is given to the church of Christ to preach, teach, baptize, and celebrate the meal. Yet the church has always deemed the ordering of this ministry as necessary for the sake of the gospel, although churches have argued as to why it is necessary and how ordered ministry serves the gospel. In fact, even churches that eschew the notion of ordered ministry do order ministry in some fashion or another.

It seems best to be self-reflective about why we engage in an ordering of ministry, and what this does and does not entail. At the risk of sounding programmatic, let me suggest three points of discussion.

First, stewardship is in the first instance a thoroughly singular task given the church, because it is finally a body, rather than a sum of bodies. Second, this stewardship is necessarily administered by some members, rather than by all, because the wisdom of God has determined that some members receive grace by celebrating word and sacrament, and some receive grace by making that celebration possible. Third, the image of stewardship alone allows order without dominance.

Stewardship is first a singular task, because it is given to the church to work in harmony according to its unity, or catholicity. Stewardship is catholic, because the church is one under the lordship of Christ. That lordship does not preclude a variety of ways of experiencing the church's catholic stewardship, yet insofar as what we steward is singular, there can be only one steward. The church as a singularity is called to be the steward of grace, because grace is one. Consequently, there is only one steward—the church. We, as individuals, are stewards by being members of this body.

The pastoral significance of starting with the catholicity of stewardship cannot be gainsaid. Stewardship is a task we engage in communally. Yet within this community, this same stewardship is differently received.

Being members of the body of Christ entails unity in diversity. This is the most significant lesson of the body-of-Christ language used in the New Testament. Even a cursory reading of the New Testament evidences a division of labor, though not in the sense that some give birth while others are born. That is the most parochial interpretation of the biblical metaphor, and is finally a betrayal of it. It is decidedly not the case that some members are important because others need them more than they themselves are needed. The tendency to see ordination as a step up a spiritual ladder betrays this presupposition. The biblical model of stewardship turns this notion on its head, insofar as it reminds us that we are blessed in our need, because it is our need that draws us into community. We need differently, and the gifts we are given testify to the shape of our need. Defining stewardship with respect to need saves us from understanding our giftedness as something we possess and over which we preside. The ordained, like the lay, have been given a gift that is first a need. Ordination, at one level, simply identifies those who have been given one set of needs rather than another. More important is the fact that the ordained and lay need one another, which leads us to our third consideration.

Stewardship is the only means by which we can distinguish lay from clergy without introducing dominance. The minister who gives what is not his or hers to give can hardly claim superiority over those who receive. Likewise, the layperson who receives gifts from the Lord via the minister sees in the minister one through whom God works for the good of the community. In our sin, we undermine this give and take in manifold ways. Some prefer a model of ministry in which professionalism is the paradigm, because this allows either the minister or the congregation to exercise the clinical objectivity that serves both parties well in dispute. Some prefer a model of ministry in which the minister is indistinguishable from members of the congregation, because this model is supposed to preclude the possibility of dominance. Some prefer a parochial model of ministry that gives the minister near-absolute power, because they believe authority can be authentically exercised only where it is given free (or nearly free) rein.

In contrast to all of these models, sacramental stewardship points to the necessarily diffuse nature of authority in the body of Christ and the necessity of locating that power in an office with clearly defined parameters. Ministers, both ordered and lay, minister according to the grace given them, and this ministry reflects the mutuality of need (Rom 12:4). There is plenty of room to discern a plurality of possibilities for imagining the concreteness of this relationship, but in each instance, the gospel undermines dominance by underlining that the need to minister is as great as the need to receive ministry, and is therefore a gift that establishes community. Yet we know this gift that is the community is not a self-referential community. The stewardship of this body that is corporate exists for the sake of God's all-embracing mission. The church exists to serve the world, so we will now consider the task of stewarding the world.

STEWARDING THE WORLD

In a sense, we return now to the beginning of this chapter. To steward the body presumes an understanding of the body as our first encounter with the world. When I steward myself, I am already stewarding the world.

Yet both the individual and the church need to attend especially to the call to steward the world at large in a time such as this. The globe is increasingly under assault by technology run amok. We cannot afford to neglect our task to exercise a respectful dominion over this gift given us. Yet if we are to properly exercise this respect, both the individual and the church must ponder our postures toward the world. This is especially true in light of the ambiguity that sometimes attends our reception of the world. What will mark our apprehension of our task as stewards in and of the world?

God loves the world. In spite of the manifold things said about the world in Scripture, within the church this must be both the starting point and the end point of our apprehension of the world. In baptism and Eucharist, in fact, the church holds the world's beginning and end in its hands. Baptism as an eternal moment recalls the genesis of the world. This birth of the world echoes the rebirth that is God's design, or end, for creation, which is communicated in Holy Communion. The sacrament of the altar gives us a foretaste of that for which creation groans in travail (Rom 8:22). Between these two sacraments, the proclamation of the word points in both directions by pointing to Christ as the one whose presence at the sacraments effects new creation. In short, the church concerns itself with the world because the church was born to bless the world. The relationship between the two is inextricable.

Contemporary Christianity in certain guises (both liberal and conservative) stigmatizes the relationship between church and world by narrating it as ever and only in conflict. Many take it for granted that this is how church and world relate. In my estimation, it is never good to take the relationship between church and world—in any guise—for granted. Querying the relationship between church and world usurps our tendency to domesticate the two.[4] But the means for unsettling a ready-made definition of the relationship between church and world is determinative for a healthy stewardship of the world.

Stewards of the world confront caricatures of church/world relationships. If the world is likened to the body, in some perverse platonic paradigm, then we simply await the moment to rid ourselves of it, so we can attain the pure being that remains unattainable by the stuff of the world. This take is seen in certain churches. The world, like the body, is considered bad, so the church really ought to have nothing to do with politics, economics, or justice. For people of this persuasion, the church dare not sully its lily-white hands with the muck of life. The church is understood to be a refuge from the world.

We also see the opposite situation. Sometimes the church seems to take its marching orders from culture. One of the most poignant examples of this was the facile manipulation of the so-called "German Christians"[5] dur-

---

4. In Lutheran circles, this tendency is most frequently seen in a misconstrual of Luther's treatment of the two reigns.

5. The "German Christians" were those Christians in Germany who acquiesced to Nazi rule.

ing Hitler's rule. When it attains a too-easy harmony with the world, the church is robbed of the ability to speak of the ambiguity of the world narrated by Scripture.

How, then, can the relationship between church and world be understood in a way that clarifies the church's responsibility toward the world, as well as the gift that the world is for the church?

We can move toward this goal by recognizing that the world is in the church and the church is in the world. At a fundamental level, it is a self-evident truth that the world is in the church, insofar as we who are embodied are the world, and we are in the church. The world is in the church as long as we grant that the church is composed of flesh-and-blood disciples of Jesus. The world is in the church in all its glory and horror—in the shadow of the fall and in the light of the eschaton.

What does this mean for the church? It means the church is a church of sinners. Our redemption is eschatologically conditioned, so we know the distinctions of sacred and profane are drawn within the church, and not at its door. Yet to speak of this alone is to speak too negatively of this relationship. The placing of the world within the church is a cause for rejoicing, too, since God made and loves the world. Our mission is in our midst, and our mission is a yoke that bears us. What first appears to be a burden is finally experienced as a blessing. The church is called to celebrate the presence of the world in the church, at the same time as it recognizes that the church is in the world.

The church *is* in the world. This is inescapable insofar as the church is composed of flesh-and-blood disciples of Jesus who exercise their vocations outside the confines of church walls. We are in the world because this is where God has called us to be. Moreover, the church is not simply in the world as a group of pious yet clandestine believers. Hopefully, disciples engage their vocation in such a way that their dealings with the world reflect the Way. The church is in the world in the mode of proclamation, and is therefore also in the world incipiently. The world, in a fashion, is pregnant with the church. The world births the church insofar as her members are incubated in the world while they await their rebirth.

This truth can and should engender a posture of gratitude toward the world. In the economy of God, creation is the condition for the possibility of re-creation. It should hasten our commitment to strive for the world's well-being. The world is not mere stuff, best abandoned in a journey toward the spiritual. The world is the locus of our ordinary lives. One of the most significant offerings of the Reformation was affirmation of the ordinary.[6] The world is where we exercise our vocation. This is true for both ordered and lay disciples. The world beckons us, because the world is where grace is already at work, drawing us and others into God's reign. Christians affirm the world, because the world is thick with God.

Still, a word of warning begs attention. The glory and horror of the human includes a propensity to extend the bit of the world that is our bodies. Technology is the means by which I can be more than I am. By way of technology, my voice travels across the oceans. By means of motors, I can outstrip the power of many horses. Because of technology, I can move faster, work harder, and live

6. See Taylor, *Sources of the Self*, 211–33.

longer than my ancestors. This gift of technology is both a bane and a blessing. The same computer that allows me to connect with people on the other side of the world can give me license to avoid face-to-face contact with people I do not much like. "The Sorcerer's Apprentice" is an apt parable of the blessings and banes of technology, and a lesson the church, too, needs to learn.

The world wherein the church is found and the world within the church beckon us to tend this dual-natured technology with care. As stewards of body, church, and world, we are called to exercise the wisdom of Solomon and the humility of Mary in order to engage the world prophetically. This is the task that most presses the church in a time such as ours, and one that reminds us that it is given to us to steward the body.

The church and its members are together given the task of stewarding the body. This means stewarding the body proper, the body of Christ, and the world of which both are instances. At the heart of this task is the Great Commission, which enjoins us to be about the task of making disciples by going into the world and meeting stewards-in-the-making, who revel in the baptismal life that flows from and leads into a life of learning.

We turn next to consideration of this task in stewarding the gospel.

6

Stewardship of Education: Teaching to Learn

GIVEN THE FACT THAT Jesus is the most often-named teacher in the Gospels, we might query the wisdom of applying such an august title to ourselves. Yet the steward of the gospel cannot prescind from making sense of this fundamental description of the teaching office entrusted to the church and its members. Our Lord commands his disciples, "Go and baptize all nations, teaching them to obey all that I have commanded you, and lo, I am with you to the end of the ages" (Matt 28:19). Teaching is described as one of the gifts of the Spirit, so it is clear that the task of teaching is entrusted to both the church and certain of her members.

In this chapter we will consider this imperative, first taking into account teaching as a function of the proclamatory task of the church, then looking at ways we learn through teaching. Teaching is learning in another mode. It provides the tools and engenders in the disciple a hunger for learning. The stewardship postures of awe and expectation challenge the standard understanding of education in the parish as the imparting of information necessary for church members to receive communion responsibly, sit on church councils, and so on. A theology of stewardship invites us to see the world differently, to imagine that education is a joy in the Christian life.

Our journey in Christ comes with the expectation that education will continuously prod, provoke, change, and delight stewards of the gospel, who confess that Christ is the teacher in whom and from whom we both teach and learn.

PREACHING AND TEACHING

Jesus's injunction to teach is given in the Great Commission:

> Now the eleven disciples went to Galilee, to the mountain to which Jesus had directed them. When they saw him, they worshipped him; but some doubted. And Jesus came and said to them, "All authority in heaven and on earth has been given to me. Go therefore and make disciples of all nations, baptizing them in the name of the Father and of the Son and of the Holy Spirit, and teaching them to obey everything that I have commanded you. And remember, I am with you always, to the end of the age." (Matt 28:16–20)

It is important to note that the Great Commission relates baptism and teaching. Teaching is not only what happens after preaching the gospel, it *is* preaching the gospel, yet in a particular way, within particular vistas of opportunity. The word preached from the pulpit reaches those anxious to feed on the bread of life. The word taught in the classroom meets the need of those who the water of life has made learners. Both modes of evangelical activity are framed by the sacramental life of the church. Teaching primarily points to a baptismal existence, just as preaching primarily points to a eucharistic ethic. We will return to the latter in the next chapter, but a few words about the former are in order now.

Teaching points us toward a baptismal life. In the life of the early church, this was evidenced by the fact that catechesis was the primary mode of education. Yet this practice is not so distant from the contemporary church. In churches that practice the ritual of confirmation, preparation for affirmation of the baptismal vows remains a primary teaching moment. Insofar as baptism is seen as an eternal event, ever active in the believer's life, the teaching ministry, as ordered toward the baptismal life, is always necessary. Gospel catechesis is ordered toward and from immersion in baptismal waters. It is part of our daily life, as we follow Luther's injunction to return to the waters of life every day.

Learning, however, presumes a teacher. Who is to teach? A clarion call to learn has not yet clarified who ought to teach, and with what sort of authority.

This worry is replicated throughout the church in a variety of ways. It is best clarified with respect to the sacramental act that teaching references: baptism itself. Who is to baptize?

The baptismal theology of many churches unequivocally confesses that God is the active agent of baptism. God alone forgives sin. God alone gives the Holy Spirit. God alone grants life eternal. God alone makes the body into a temple. These truths are axiomatic for the freshly minted pastor who pours water for the first time in the name of the Father, and the Son, and the Holy Spirit. "Can it be," he or she asks, "that I am the hand of the Lord? Why me?" This is one of the most important questions asked within the church, a question guided by Luther's treatment of the so-called priesthood of all believers.

Luther's treatment of the common priesthood helps us recognize that because Christ alone is properly *the* priest, the church errs wholly when it affirms either the priesthood of some believers or the priesthood of each believer. The former error allows some to think they have a divine grace that is not proper to the community. The latter allows others to imagine that this same grace is parceled out in piecemeal fashion to every Christian. The former represents the worst of hierarchal ecclesiology. The latter represents the marriage of civil religion and market economics. Both fall far from the common priesthood as Luther imagined it.

The priesthood of all believers begins with the affirmation that God in Christ is priest, a theme developed in the book of Hebrews. Priesthood is predicated of believers, because they are members of the body of Christ. Our priesthood occurs by our participation in Christ, and is thereby a derived priesthood. He who is priest promises his presence at each community gathering around word and sacrament, for the sake of the world. Each sacramental event in the life of the community is an instantiation of Christ, present at the Eucharist and embodied in our sacramental activities.

Yet the nature of a ministry of word and sacrament demands that a voice be heard—and heard in concert with other voices, which represent both the breadth and the charisms of the community. That voice is the voice of the pastor. In the call to be pastor, the charisms given the church are concretized in one of the baptized. The charisms meet the church's recognition of this person as one called to serve Christ's church. This individual speaks the gospel to and on behalf of the community, so the community can live the gospel in the world. The priesthood of all believers recognizes the ordered ministry as a condition for its possibility.

A parallel situation obtains with respect to the teacher.

All teachers of Christ teach, by virtue of their participation in Christ. Christ is our rabbi. Just as some are ordered to preach to the community so that the community can minister in the world, some are called to teach the community so that all may both teach and learn in the world.

This presumes that the relationship between teacher and learner is something other than that between an expert and an empty vessel waiting to be filled. The relationship between teacher and learner is first and foremost a mystery, bound by a mutual need. The student is patently dependent upon the teacher, who has been habituated in the art of learning the particular subject matter.[1] The teacher is latently dependent on the student, who evokes the passion that makes possible further learning for the teacher. Teacher and student meet in this mutuality of need. Teaching is therefore an exercise in vulnerability.[2] This vulnerability is safeguarded from abuse when the heart of the teacher-student relationship is the subject

---

1. Jacques Barzun notes that one teaches a student how to learn a subject, rather than teaching the subject per se. See Barzun, *Begin Here*, 35.

2. Palmer, *The Courage to Teach*, 17.

matter. Neither student nor teacher has pride of place, as Parker Palmer has so eloquently demonstrated.[3]

While this is clearly true for all teaching, there is something peculiar about this truth as it applies to the topic of teaching the faith. If a subject matter of any kind draws a student and teacher into a relationship, then a student and teacher are especially interdependent when the subject matter is God. And when teacher and learner are enchanted by the subject matter that is the gospel, not only are they drawn outside of themselves, they are—more important—drawn into the world.[4] Teaching is part and parcel of the *missio Dei* (mission of God).

The Great Commission points to the world as the place where we learn, for the sake of the world. Yet not only do we learn for the world, we also learn from the world. This theme will be illumined in the next section, after we consider how "teaching to learn" refers to teaching as learning in another mode.

TEACHING AS LEARNING

Many people have discovered that by teaching a subject, they have finally begun to learn it. The pastor who knows someone in his or her adult Bible class might ask about the economic practices of first-century Palestine will be driven to fill out crevices of ignorance that might otherwise be overlooked.

Teaching is a mode of learning, because in teaching the teacher discovers the wonder of learning—a wonder

---

3. Palmer, *The Courage to Teach*, 116.

4. Barzun notes that the virtue of learning is the fact that it takes one out of oneself and into a subject. See *Begin Here*, 44.

that echoes the baptismal posture of astonishment we discussed in the first chapter. In a fundamental way, teaching leads the teacher to the threshold of the miracle of thought. She sees it in the faces of students that light up with the arrival of a new concept. From time to time, he feels it in his own face, as a vista of possibilities arrive in the space created by the question of a student who cleverly—even if unintentionally—reveals a crack in an argument and blows a subject open in a new way. In the give and take of question and answer, of prod and poke, ideas are born. The teacher discovers anew the wonder that thought is how the mind creates. Just as the potter needs clay, the teacher needs questions, to think, create, synthesize. The student is the gift of the question, evoking the activity of thinking, complete with all the labor pains that attend the exhilarating arrival of an idea. Thought is no less a miracle than birth, because thought and birth are kin—both are God's creative activity extended into our sometimes mundane yet meaningful world. The steward, as one who lives in awe and expectation, can expect to be intrigued by teaching, learning, and the fascinating interdependence of the two. He or she is astounded by the mysterious manner in which learning advances. This mystery itself bears witness to the riches of a life of faith.

Although intrigued by the wonder of learning, a steward of the gospel is not naïve about learning. Learning is a wonder, yet it is also hard work. Knowing how is a step on the way to knowing what and asking why.[5] For those

---

5. Regan, *Toward an Adult Church*, 77–78.

Stewardship of Education: Teaching to Learn

who persevere in the gift of learning and teaching, it is no surprise that education is sometimes called an art.[6]

But what is an art?

"Art," of course, is one of those slippery words that sometimes invite people to foist meanings onto them. For this discussion, let me propose that art is marked by the activity of attending to the particular in the whole, and to the whole in the particular.[7] Picasso's painting *Guernica* is a response to the German bombing in the Basque region as ordered by Franco, yet it is more than that. It portrays the universal experience of the anguish of betrayal and senseless suffering. In a rather opposite manner, one cannot look upon the various ancient depictions of the three graces (beauty, charm, and joy) without imagining how the things that bring us truth, beauty, and goodness draw from and empower one another. Art attends to the whole in the part, and to the part in the whole.

But how does one arrive at art, and how does one evaluate art? These are pressing questions if teaching is an art!

In contemporary parlance, one is wont to use language of intuition to describe the work of artists, in contradistinction to the work of scientists, which deals in matters of fact, reason, and quantification. While this way of speaking seems commonsensical to most of us, the difficulty it poses is evident when we ask someone what "intuition" means. This word is difficult to define. If teaching is an art, and art depends on intuition, and we have trouble defining intuition, then we are in sore straits!

6. Barzun, *Begin Here*, 5.
7. Schleiermacher, *Dialectic*, 4.

In ancient thought, "intuition" had a specific meaning: it was a mode of knowing restricted to angels. Mortals knew things by way of trial and error, complete with the sensual give and take of perception and misperception, and the subsequent intellectual struggle of making sense of what they saw, heard, and so on. Angels had things easier. Mortals came to realization of the Pythagorean formula by trial and error. Angels just knew this truth; it came to them immediately from God. Mortals knew by the hard work of thought; angels knew with neither struggle nor stages. Mortals knew over time; angels knew instantly, by intuition.

We probably can't work with this idea of intuition, though it does point us to an important theme in the art of teaching to learn.

What most people mean by "intuition" today might better be called "a hunch."[8] A hunch is a vague sense that something is around the corner, something I ought to attend to, something that will demand my attention. Artists, as well as scientists, work with hunches.

Of course, the hunch does not preclude the importance of plain old hard work. The artist depends on the hunch because it has been shaped and formed by the hard work of being schooled in how to look. We often speak of what to look for, but we too rarely speak of how to look. We need to look expectantly, patiently, carefully, and with wonder. Art demands such an eye. Teaching demands such an eye, such an ear. Teaching the self how to listen and how to see is the first step to teaching, period.[9]

---

8. See Taylor, *A Secular Age*, 550.
9. Palmer, *Courage to Teach*, 112–13.

Stewardship of Education: Teaching to Learn

We see a fine example of this in Jesus's interactions with a lawyer in Luke 10: 25–37. In this passage, he employs the parable of the Good Samaritan. Many of us know the story well. A lawyer wants to justify himself, so Jesus tells this beloved story that demonstrates that the neighbor is who God puts in our path.

Another important lesson is found in the passage leading up to the parable. We read in Luke 10:25–28:

> Just then a lawyer stood up to test Jesus. "Teacher," he said, "what must I do to inherit eternal life?" He said to him, "What is written in the law? What do you read there?" He answered, "You shall love the Lord your God with all your heart, and with all your soul, and with all your strength, and with all your mind; and your neighbor as yourself." And he said to him, "You have given the right answer; do this and you will live."

Unfortunately, English versions of this passage miss an important insight afforded us in the Greek original. While the English translation reads "What do you read there?" the Greek original reads "How do you read?" There is a startling difference between these two translations. The question "how?" invites the reader to understand that the reader brings a perspective to the text that affects how he or she reads. Jesus invited the lawyer, and invites us as well, to consider what presuppositions we bring to the task of reading, as well as to the task of learning. Those who learn and teach in awe and expectation are shaped by a curiosity and wonder that enliven their learning experience.

Teaching to learn is possible only because we have first been taught how to learn, and we take that inquisitive capacity into every activity that occupies us—especially, and most important, into teaching itself. Those who teach to learn enter the classroom with the expectation that what will transpire may be a delight, or a disaster, or a bit of both, but that as long as we have ears, teaching is an opportunity to learn. The learning might not always please us, but for teachers motivated to learn, this is never as immobilizing as not learning at all. By God's grace, every teaching event is an opportunity to learn, and therefore an immersion into the wonder of God's richness.

But learning is not an easily acquired habit. Those who teach to learn also have to teach others how to learn. We will now consider this task.

ENGENDERING PATTERNS OF CURIOSITY

Jane Regan notes that being conditioned to see the world in a certain way is both a blessing and a bane. The prejudices that shape our apprehensions of this world are both necessary and restricting.[10] We see what we have been trained to see, which both blinds us and opens our eyes.

In my year of internship as a pastor, I took an art class. We learned to look for reflection of color on items where we would not normally expect to see reflections. So when I drove on the gray highway in summer, I could see green and blue in varying strengths on the road. In the fall, I could see yellow and orange from the trees mixing with sky blue on the highway. I had not noticed this until I was told to look for it, at which point it become obvious. If you are painting a portrait of a woman wearing a red shirt, the shadow on the underside of her face has hues of red. I learned to see differently when I saw through paint.

10. Regan, *Adult Church*, 80.

Stewardship of Education: Teaching to Learn

I also learn to see differently through stewardship. Teaching and education have profoundly different hues as a result of the baptismal astonishment that we *are* rather than we *are not*; that God loves us for the sake of the world, which we are and we are not; that God's grace of re-creation is evident in creation, for those who have been given the eye to see it. Teaching to learn is one of the most significant ways God gives us such an eye. But such a conversion invites a revolution in our perception of perception itself.

Medieval theology wisely distinguished the human patient from the agent. The patient was the recipient of action, the agent the doer. If you do something to me, you are the agent, and I am the patient. Humans are agents and patients both. Modern thought is not so far removed from this, although we may use different language to make these distinctions. An important difference is our perception of the senses. Common sense might inform us that we are wholly patients with regard to our senses. What I see, hear, feel, smell, and taste are largely at the mercy of the external world, which impinges on me. At a fundamental level, this is true, and was recognized by the ancients. Yet they said more, which we will consider with a richer phenomenology of seeing in this chapter and of hearing in the next.

Medieval theologians and philosophers considered sight one of the primary ways we apprehend the external world. Among them, some followed Plato's teaching of extramission, believing that when a person saw an object, rays reached out from his or her eyes and apprehended the object, much the same way as my fingers reach out and tell me something about the shape of whatever I feel. This contrasts with the modern view of the physiology of sight, which explains that light enters my eyes and traces patterns on my retinas, which communicate those patterns to my brain via nerve signals. These ancient thinkers had an altogether different understanding of sight. For them, sight was not a wholly passive activity. Of course, that is also true, to a degree, in contemporary understanding: we can choose to look—or not—at what attracts, intrigues, disgusts, or bores us. But the ancients who affirmed extramission went a step further. The eyes connected with their objects by reaching into the world. Seeing the world was being in the world. In some interesting ways, such truths are being rediscovered by modern science.

What bearing does this have on the task of teaching to learn?

As long as we envision our seeing as wholly disengaged and distant, we imagine that we can be neutral observers of the world. Seers who touch the world, however, are thrust into a kind of relationship that entails commitment. This commitment presumes a sharing of the self that is best described as a vulnerability involving reciprocity. When I know more about climate change, I apprehend my world and my place in it differently. More important, when I approach the world with intentionality in my seeing, I discover that the world is richer and more diverse than I first expected.

Realizing this drives us to a fundamental theme that presents itself when we first think about learning: the phenomenon of nescience, or of not knowing.

To know, in the first instance, always takes place against the horizon of not knowing. We learn this phenomenon quickly when we discover the breadth of possibilities that open before us with a little knowledge. At first,

Stewardship of Education: Teaching to Learn

this experience can be dizzying and exciting. But as we continue in our educational venture, this dizzying experience can become frightening, perhaps even terrorizing. This is evident in the experience of graduate students. As they prepare theses and dissertations, the lists of materials they really ought to master grows exponentially with every book they read. Their must-read lists are endless. At a fundamental level, all humans know this—not only graduate students. This knowledge sometimes activates a kind of brake on learning.

In teaching to learn, we must address this phenomenon, or fear will frustrate our engagement with the world. We must learn (and teach our students) how to deal with the fear of nescience, of not knowing. We must embrace our fear. Not knowing is rather like death: just as death is not erased by our refusal to recognize it, so nescience will not go away by our refusal to face it. Just as death presses upon life and so shapes it, because it is a part of life, so not knowing is part and parcel of knowing. Not knowing is the limit that announces that I am in a world I cannot fully apprehend. Not knowing finally announces that I am not God.

At a fundamental level, then, my refusal to embrace my nescience and my reticence to open myself to the world represents a kind of idolatry, and therefore a refusal to be a steward. In my fear of not knowing, I prefer a world circumscribed by my own expertise, where I can be a master. Embracing nescience unmasks and addresses my fear.

This fear to learn has too successfully set the agenda for education within the church. Education becomes a task that can be mastered, rather than an art that invites lifelong delight. Education is framed by fear—fear of change, fear of failure, and fear of not knowing. Fear paralyzes the church.

How is such fear to be addressed theologically?

First, we need to embrace our fear of not knowing, just as we embrace our fear of death. After embracing such a fear, we recognize that just as God baptismally engages death for the sake of life, he also baptismally engages nescience for the sake of knowing, and fear for the sake of faith. Nescience, in fact, shapes us as knowers by engendering in us a kind of humility that is conditional for learning. Humility is the ground out of which learning grows. The disciple advances in faith by facing the fear entailed in not knowing.

Not knowing is not just negative. There is also a certain freedom in recognizing that I cannot know all. When I embrace nescience, I am freed from the responsibility of knowing all, and this freedom *from* becomes a freedom *for* knowing that allows me to enter more deeply into my world. We must understand this as concretely as possible. Just as the command to love thy neighbor is possible only when a real neighbor is intended, so knowing the world is possible only in the face of the world with which we are most intimate.

In the last chapter, we noted that this bit of the world is my body, and beyond this, I am called to know the world of my neighborhood. Learning to know first invites me to look more closely at the world within my proximity. I am also invited to know something of the cosmos writ large—which begins from knowing who, what, and where I am. This knowing, on a micro scale, awakens within me a wonder and delight in all experiences of knowing. The task of teaching to learn is not so much about developing techniques or strategies for continuing education—although it may involve that. More important, teaching to learn involves birthing (gendering) in (en) students a passionate interest in the world around them.

What does engendering a passion for learning mean for life in a parish?

A parish that takes both stewardship and education seriously acknowledges that religious education is not just about giving children facts through a Sunday-school-and-confirmation regime that ends in a "graduation." Our theology of stewardship recognizes that stewards are shaped by an astonishment and expectation that invite us to pursue our passions as we draw ever more deeply into the mystery who is God. Education is the means by which we are drawn out of ourselves, and through which a vision for the common weal of the world is engendered in us. For this reason, education is at the heart of parish life, because it is a mode of word and sacrament.

How can parishes be released from a too-common understanding of church education that is parallel to the worst of school mentality, which aims merely at graduation? This is a more pressing, complicated problem than it might appear, since the habit of learning is both taught and caught. Our churches are not full of people who effuse the curiosity that leads to education.

Our situation is a variant of the dilemma facing indigenous Canadians. Beginning in the late nineteenth century, in an effort to assimilate them into broader Canadian culture, the government forced native Canadians to send their children to residential schools run by the government and by churches who acted as agents for the government. The tragic legacy of this policy was a generation of indigenous people who were raised by institutions rather than by their parents. These children, in turn, became unparented parents. Not only were these residential students not habituated in aboriginal ways of parenting and living, they also passed on their losses to subsequent generations. First Nations people are now making great strides in correcting this injustice, which left a mass legacy of loss.[11]

Institutions, including the church, often suffer legacies of loss in a parallel manner. From generation to generation, the church has failed to see education for what it is. Instead, it has seen Christian education as a stepping stone to full involvement in the church, supposing that the baptized who have not yet been confirmed are pre-members of the church. Individuals have had to be confirmed, to receive communion and serve on church committees. Education has been rendered a condition to be fulfilled for a greater end. Education in this guise has been a legacy that cannot be easily overcome.

Our one saving grace may be that the church is dying, and in resurrecting it, God brings into our fold people who do not share an institutional memory of education as a means to an end. Some of these people come with a fierce hunger for Christian education, because they know it is of a piece with word and sacrament. They encounter Jesus in learning. They may be able to teach us to learn by reminding us that education is not just an end, but also a means. Moreover, its end is our participation in Christ's kenotic, self-giving posture. Education draws us out of

---

11. You can read about this process at Truth and Reconciliation Canada's website. See also King, *The Truth about Stories,* and Tinker, *American Indian Liberation.*

ourselves into the world, where we not only teach, but also learn.

Calvin famously spoke of the Scriptures as spectacles, enabling us to see the world differently.[12] He understood that the Christian who sees the world through the lens of Scripture is able to see creation praising God. The gospel enables us to approach creation with a posture of curiosity. We lean in for a closer look at creation and culture both, looking for footprints with nail-shaped holes. We look for God in the world, because our sacred story reminds us that God both created and loved the world. We seek signs of God because we have been made curious, and the curious cast caution to the wind when they are hot on the trail of the divine. The world makes our hearts pound, because even in the midst of its deprivation—and there is more than a little of that—we find God. Our children need to see this passion in us—or, more likely, we need to see this passion in and learn from our children. Children are sometimes able to teach us to learn, which brings us to a closing reflection before we consider the proclamation of stewardship.

In my denomination, children's sermons have become de rigueur. In fact, certain parishes expect pastors to do children's sermons even when no are children present.

I am now convinced that many children's sermons are not for the children at all. In some instances, the concepts presented are too abstract; in other instances, children take over the show and incite giggling and "ohs" and "ahs" from the people in the pews. Perhaps this is how it should be. Maybe adults need this. I'm not sure the chil-

12. Calvin, *Institutes of the Christian Religion*, 70.

dren do. But what does strike me as hopeful is the way adults are transfixed by children's curiosity. They love the way a child whose view is obscured by someone's shoulder will stand on her toes and push her nose around a corner to get a glimpse of what is going on that she cannot see. The children are not getting a sermon, so much as giving a sermon. They incarnate the gospel depiction of the reign of God: Zacchaeus climbing a tree to see our Lord; the woman searching high and low for the lost coin; Jesus seeing and showing signs in creation and culture that remind his hearers that God is in the midst of the ordinary. For those given eyes to see, losing decorum for a pearl of wisdom is a small price of admission to glimpses of God. If children can teach us this, these so-called sermons are worth keeping.

The Great Commission commits the church to the task of learning and teaching. In the process, we enter into the baptismal life that establishes a posture of astonishment and awe in stewards of the gospel. Yet those who stand in awe are also on the lookout. We live in eucharistic expectation, which has a particular connection with the task of preaching in the life of the church.

We will now consider this in relationship to stewardship of the gospel.

7

Proclaiming Stewardship and a Stewardship of Proclamation

IN THIS CHAPTER, WE first explore the relationship of stewardship to proclamation, examining how a compelling and vital proclamation of stewardship requires that we first be stewards of proclamation itself. We will consider how both preacher and hearer are faithful stewards of the Word of God by speaking, hearing, and living in awe and expectation.

Preaching, of course, is one of the constitutive moments in the life of the church. At the Eucharist, stewards of the gospel come to anticipate that they will now receive personally the word they hear publically. Luther said it best:

> But when I distribute the sacrament, I designate it for the individual who is receiving it; I give him Christ's body and blood, that he may have forgiveness of sins, obtained through his death and preached in the congregation. This is something more than the congregational sermon; for although the same thing is present in the sermon as in the sacrament, here there is the advantage that it is directed at definite individuals. In the sermon one does not point out or portray any particular person, but in the sacrament it is given

to you and to me in particular, so that the sermon comes to be our own.[1]

Luther sees an intimate connection between the sermon and Holy Communion. Each informs the other. The sermon provides the hearer with the content of the gospel, and Eucharist gives occasion for the steward to personally hear the words "given for you." Stewards of the gospel, then, hear the sermon in the posture of expectation the Eucharist shapes in us.

In considering the place of the sermon in a stewardship of the gospel, we will explore what a stewardship of proclamation itself might look like, then consider what it means to proclaim stewardship themes in the life of the parish.

THE STEWARDSHIP OF PROCLAMATION

We are all well aware of the task of proclaiming stewardship. Some of the stewardship we have proclaimed or heard proclaimed might have sorely vexed us. It is my contention that those vexing occasions reflect an inadequate theology of proclamation, representing a failure to see proclamation itself as an instance of stewardship. For those of us who are preachers, this might seem so self-evident as to be a truism. After all, we are to be stewards of time, treasure, and talent, and most pastors consider preaching one of their talents.

But for those of us who are hearers, the notion of a stewardship of proclamation might seem applicable to preachers alone. This distinction between hearer and preacher is not so clear as we might imagine. We who are

1. Luther, "The Sacrament of the Body and Blood of Christ," 348.

preachers of the word are also hearers of the word, and those of us who are hearers of the word often unknowingly hear our own voices reflected in the words of proclamation. Pastors, after all, proclaim in contexts shaped by our hearers. Proclamation at its best is a dialogue—or, better yet, a trialogue. The minister of the word attends to both the sacred text and the given context, and adds his or her own subtext to the sermon. These three voices meet in the sermon, and both the speaker and hearer, by the grace of the word of God, are able to receive this word in awe and expectation. This grace makes us response-able. Moreover, grace itself determines that kenosis, or self-emptying, constitutes the core of our response to grace.

Kenosis is the Jesus way of living together in community.[2] Kenosis points to the manner of being by which the first become last and the last become first. Kenosis describes the trinitarian decision to be self-giving. Both creation and redemption refer to God's self-giving manner of being. This manner of being can be described only as gracious. To be gracious is to give, and to be a steward is to participate in this mode of being. Stewards achieve plenitude only by generosity. This is as true of proclamation as it is of all time, treasure, and talent. We achieve our goal of self-realization by divesting ourselves of ourselves. And the means by which we do this is communication.

What do I mean by this?

Communication is a critical aspect of human existence. Unfortunately, it is increasingly understood under a technical rather than an organic paradigm.

---

2. See footnote 44 in chapter 5 for a definition of "kenotic," which is the adjectival form of the noun "kenosis," derived from the Greek verb for "to empty."

A technical paradigm of communication understands it as a means whereby data are transferred from one to the other. Communication, in this paradigm, merely describes the means by which we pass something to someone else. What we pass may vary. It might be details regarding the weather. It might be the state of my financial portfolio. It might be important information about this or that. What we give are data, and the sharing of data is inconsequential to our existence. A computer shares files without loss. When this becomes the operative paradigm for thinking about all communication, we imagine that we can inform other people without consequence for our own being. All I give is information.

This is different from an organic model of communication, in which we do not share information—we share ourselves. In organic communication, we give something of ourselves. The paradigm for this model is the incarnation, death, and resurrection of Christ. Christological communication is kenotic. The event of Christ has been described as the self-communication of God. When the Word became flesh, we were not given facts; we were given God's very self. Self-communication is the model whereby we understand organic communication.

There is an inherent risk in organic communication. When I share something of myself with others, I do not know what will come of it. People might abuse me, or ignore me, or embrace me. The mark of authentic communication is actual giving of the self. A kind of loss is involved in this. I am, in some sense, lessened by this kenotic offer. I reveal what is hidden in me; I give it away. Authentic communication is revelatory. The mystery that I am is made available to others.

And that is what most frightens us about the prospect of organic communication: we have no clue what will come of our self-disclosure. This anxiety is compounded by our concern that what we have communicated might be misunderstood. How many of us have shared things with others, only to discover that what we said and what they heard were two different things?

There are two responses to this dilemma. We either revert to technical communication or we dare to die by speaking authentically. We take control, or we take risks. One way or the other. The first is the way of manipulative management. The second is the way of stewardship.

Stewardship of proclamation is a path of risk. It is daring to share ourselves with others by authentically giving of ourselves in proclamation. This makes demands on both speakers and hearers. When proclamation is crafted by stewardship, the speaker gives him or herself in the sermon. This might involve sharing a personal story. It might involve risking an untested idea. It might involve using a new way of preaching, or preaching from a different location, or setting aside notes, or perhaps starting to use notes! Proclamation is owned kenotically only when the preacher allows him or herself to be vulnerable in the sermon.[3]

It is not just the preacher who needs to be vulnerable. Hearers, too, are stewards of proclamation, by demonstrating a kind of vulnerability—but of a different sort.

Hearers of proclamation face a critical decision in the pew. We have to determine whether we will hear this

3. Vulnerability does not equate to using the pulpit as a psychologist's couch. Authentic vulnerability is a willingness to expose fear and courage, doubt and faith, weakness and strength.

sermon with the expectation that God speaks through it. If God does not speak through it, the sermon becomes an occasion for daydreaming, or for entertainment, or perhaps for information about cultural artifacts from the biblical world. But if God does speak through the sermon, a pathway that makes certain demands upon us determines our very existence. We are committed to listening expectantly for God in the sermon. This means we listen to the preacher no matter what. In the sermon, we listen not for an affirmation of our preconceived ideas, nor for advice on how to vote, nor for something that make us feel better about ourselves. We listen for the living voice of God—the *viva vox*—in, with, and under the voice of the preacher.

This all sounds good, but what if we are stuck with a preacher who is utterly dismal? What then?

The task of listening for the word of God starts prior to the sermon and ends well after the sermon ends. The whole worship service serves the proclamation of the gospel. The sermon proper is a particular and critical moment in this movement. Within the broader occasion of hearing the word, the sermon's particular task begins with the reading of the text and ends with eucharistic reception. We may feel comfortable in judging preachers irrelevant, but none of us has the authority to judge as irrelevant the word we hear or the sacrament we receive! Some dismal sermons might not be quite so dismal if they are heard within this broader context of proclamation. The opposite may also be true. In either event, a posture of expectation is decisive.

"What is God saying to me?" is not a question asked first of the sermon. It is first asked of the texts on which the sermon is based, then of the sermon proper, and finally of the Eucharist, which personalizes the word of God. The sermon gives the hearer a particular opportunity to reflect on this question.

To arrive at this point, the preacher—like the listener—has to come to grips with kenosis. Kenotic hearing is uncertain about what we need to hear. We all bring questions and concerns to the text. But as kenotic hearers, we dare to imagine that we might not know what we need to hear. Hearing is, in fact, the sine qua non (indispensable condition) of proclamation. Hearers who truly hear have forfeited control. They wait upon the word that comes to them from afar. They cannot turn the volume up; they cannot fast-forward or pause. They wait upon the word. And that is exactly what stewardship is, in its purest form.

At one level, the sermon is the instantiation par excellence of stewardship. Stewardship means hanging upon every word that comes from the mouth of God. Stewardship means living from syllable to syllable, soaking in every pause, thrilled by inflection, buoyed by intonation. Stewardship means living from God's word and hearing it expectantly, always asking, "What is God saying to me, to us?" This is the same as asking, "What is God giving of God's very self to me, to us?"

Preachers can be preachers only by hearing. And hearers of the preached word become preachers by sharing what they hear with others. Stewards of proclamation are evangelists. They give away what they hear, because they know that sharing does not deplete their account, but is the path to plenitude in the reign of God. We give up; we are kenotic in both hearing and speaking, because we know that giving is reception par excellence. We are grasped by the mystery of the reign of God.

"Mystery," of course, is a loaded word. For some folk, "mystery" means, above all, finding out what is not known. That is how the genre of mystery operates in literary circles. A mystery is marked by a problem that is hidden from view, but which can be solved. Mysteries in our world are, above all, to be solved. This is not how the word "mystery" operates in the reign of God.

Here we must return to the word's Greek origin, *muein,* "to close." This word was originally used to describe initiates, who were to close their eyes during initiation into religious cults.[4] Of course, the initiates never closed their eyes for good. Eventually they opened their eyes to partake of cult activities. Mystery is, above all else, about initiation. It is about beginning. Mysteries are not solved—that is not what they are for. Mysteries initiate us into a way of life. They make us realize that the more we know, the more we know we don't know.

Mystery therefore habituates a posture of wonder in us. Those who are drawn into the mystery of grace are astounded to discover that the more they give, the more they get—that the riches of God are inexhaustible. Mysteries are not solved, they are enduringly enjoyed. The mystery of grace invites us to expect much of proclamation, because it schools us into a posture of awe and expectation: it makes us generous. By grace through faith, we come to see that those who hoard are the poorest, because they rob themselves of the riches of God.

Those who fail to risk fail altogether, because risky speaking and risky hearing are the means whereby God

4. These cults were groups of like-minded individuals seeking religious experience using a variety of methods. "Cult" in this sense is rather different from the way we use the word today.

communicates. When God communicates, we do not receive information—we receive God. This is the truth implicit in a stewardship of proclamation.

How can this truth of the stewardship of proclamation inform the very necessary task of proclaiming stewardship?

PROCLAIMING STEWARDSHIP

Here we consider the way stewardship clarifies our human identity, as compared to the human propensity to usurp God. This will lead to a discussion of the particular problems in preaching about money. We can then comment on the need to proclaim stewardship in the life of the parish.

An idolatrous itch persists insidiously in the human heart, its ability to mask itself its greatest guile: we, who are called to serve God, wish to be like gods (Gen 3:5). This propensity lies behind human disinterest in the theme of stewardship.

Stewardship is the aspect of discipleship that confirms our identities as the Lord's servants. Stewardship is the anthropological correlate of the first commandment. The only means by which we proclaim the God of Jesus Christ as Lord of all is by asserting that we are servants of this same God. To stand in a disinterested posture is impossible, in light of God's claims. We are either for or against this God, and being for God determines our identities as stewards, even while we affirm our identities as God's sons and daughters. Being authorized to act in God's stead confirms our existence as creatures whose glory it is to serve the Lord of all creation.

This glory, however, is a reflected glory, because our identities as stewards always point attention away from ourselves, and toward the one we glorify. To be a steward is to fulfill the first commandment. To eschew stewardship is to declare divinity for the self. Stewardship is therefore at the heart of the life of discipleship. This is the reason for its problematic reception within the church. Humans invariable assert a desire "to be like" God. As long as the old Adam and Eve remain, stewardship will resolutely remain a challenge for the church. This is why stewardship simply must remain at the heart of Christian proclamation.

The church must come to grips with this state of affairs. One way it masks its idolatrous assumption of the role of master is by parceling off the themes of stewardship as though time, talent, and treasure could be understood in abstraction from one another. The commonsensical assertion that time is money discloses the impossibility of treating treasure as a necessary evil, in opposition to the charismata (gifts) of time and talent. Time, talent, and treasure exist together in a sort of interweaving, which recognizes that they are the means by which we exercise our identity as stewards. Time, talent, and treasure are the tools of the steward, each depending on the others for activation. The proclamation of stewardship demands attention to all of these elements, because one cannot exist in abstraction from the others.

In our culture, this presents a problem for addressing finances in the context of the sermon.

Many pastors in Christ's church have been raised to understand that they are to attend to things spiritual, while the church council, vestry, and board are to worry about money. Such an approach fails the church by rendering money profane. It neglects the intention of the common priesthood, which refuses to accept the division of sacred and profane as a description of the relationship of clergy to laity.

It is given to pastors to speak of money, because disciples of Jesus speak his agenda. Money was clearly of concern to our Lord. In speaking of it, he was able to order this ambiguous symbol under the power of the gospel, affirming its utility for God's reign. The preacher, then, speaks along with Jesus about money, and in so doing reclaims currency for the reign of God. Preaching this reality is rather like walking up an escalator that is moving down.

This brings us to our final reflection about proclamation of stewardship.

It is increasingly commonplace for churches to have a stewardship month. This is an important advance in church life. It moves us beyond the notion that people will give when they see or hear of a specific need. It reflects an understanding that stewardship is not just about dollars, but also about engagement of all that we are, for the sake of the gospel. Yet setting aside one month for stewardship focus can still contribute to an understanding of stewardship as a task separate from the church's life of worship.

I propose that, to understand stewardship, the church move from a project paradigm to a process paradigm.

A project paradigm of stewardship is admittedly an important advance beyond no paradigm of stewardship! Yet it has shortfalls. It may invite people to think of stewardship as one of many church activities. It may invite people to consider stewardship as an exercise in meeting budgets. It may relieve the congregation as a whole from the task of stewardship, by assigning it to a committee. I propose that the church is best served by moving from a project to a process notion of stewardship, and that preaching is an integral component of this conversion.

A process notion of stewardship begins with the assumption that stewardship is an act of worship. This is symbolized in the worship service, which incorporates offering and offertory. Yet more needs to be done within the average congregation to advance the idea that what flows into the church also flows out of the church in service to others. This is true of the money we bring to the church, of course, but it is equally true of ourselves. Worship is the process whereby stewards are transformed into agents of reconciliation in the world. The process of stewardship is grounded in word and sacrament, whereby we are changed by our giving, so we might be contagions of grace in the world. The worship function of the church must be constantly held to this task, and the sermon is an important tool in this process.

What, then, of stewardship programs and committees? Are they to be abolished?

Oddly enough, I propose that we continue with stewardship committees, and even with stewardship months. Such action can be likened to our adherence to St. Paul's admonition to pray at all times by setting aside particular times in which to pray, as our Lord taught. Likewise, stewardship committees should set aside stewardship months, to ground the whole life of the church in stewardship. In so doing, the committees will enable stewardship to inform the decisions of every committee in the church.

It is therefore imperative that stewardship remain an integral component of the homiletic task of the parish pastor. Stewardship should be on the agenda of every sermon, precisely so it gets a broader grounding in the life of the church. Setting aside special times and events is an auxiliary strategy. The notion of process does not preclude project; it orders project toward a broader mandate: to make stewardship the axis of our response to the gospel.

Stewardship is a way of life. Some, however, fear that this assertion becomes a truism, reducing the countercultural current of stewardship. Perhaps it is better to assert that stewardship is the way of death and life. The baptismal reference in this phrase becomes the operative paradigm, as we orient our lives in a response to God whereby we encounter, in mystery, the truth that giving is the mode by which we receive in God's reign. Just as baptism washes and empowers us for service, so a life of stewardship enables us to encounter the life changing power of God, so we become bearers of the power through which God changes the world.

This is the inexhaustible truth of stewardship. We, who are not lords, become the agents through whom the Lord of life exercises the love that ever expands the divine reign.

Afterword

A GOOD FRIEND OF mine, Jeff Pym, director of Lutheran Planned Giving, recently presented a seminar at a stewardship workshop entitled "Goodbye Stewardship, Hello Generosity." He reported that the seminar was largely met with respectful silence. The premise of his talk was that the genesis of stewardship in the lives of our church has been so wholly cast in language of obligation as to render "stewardship" irredeemably negative. When people hear the word "stewardship," they instinctively bury their talents.

The year before Jeff offered this seminar, he and I presented a workshop on stewardship at Waterloo Lutheran Seminary. He was working with this theme at the same time as I was writing chapter 2 of this book, in which I advance the idea that the New Testament offers two dominant images for our identity as Christians: stewards and children. We seemed to arrive at a similar theme from two directions.

Without doubt, the theme of "stewardship" can do as much harm as good: "the corruption of the best is the worst." In this book I have endeavored to reclaim the elements of a theology of stewardship that make it a useful, beneficial approach to church life. Yet as the book ends, I remind readers that stewardship is not the sum of the Christian practice under the gospel. Stewardship sheds a particular light on critical core practices within the

Afterword

church. It brings to the fore particular contours of word and sacrament, and their concretization in the church's day-to-day existence. It does not illumine every contour of church practice.

We could revisit the exercise of this book using family, citizenship, or other images to illumine other aspects of the core practices of the church. At the end of the day, however, what recommends stewardship as an important theme for church life is the fact that it moves the steward to see him or herself as child, citizen, friend, neighbor.

In the end, awe and expectation are too big to be restricted to stewardship alone, because the God who inspires awe and expectation is so much more than any one image can capture.

Bibliography

Aquinas, Thomas. *The Catechetical Instructions of St. Thomas Aquinas.* Translated with a commentary by Joseph B. Collins. Manila: Sinag-Tala, 1939.

Aristotle. *The Nicomachean Ethics.* Cambridge: Harvard University Press, 1999.

Barzun, Jacques. *Begin Here: The Forgotten Conditions of Teaching and Learning.* Edited by Morris Philipson. Chicago: University of Chicago Press, 1991.

Calvin, John. *Calvin: Institutes of the Christian Religion 1.* Vol. 20, *The Library of Christian Classics,* edited by John T. McNeill, translated and indexed by Ford Lewis Battles. Philadelphia: Westminster John Knox, 1960.

Dillard, Annie. *An American Childhood.* New York: Harper Perennial, 1987.

Evangelical Lutheran Church in America. *Evangelical Lutheran Worship.* Pew ed. Minneapolis: Fortress, 2006.

Hall, Douglas John. *The Steward: A Biblical Symbol Come of Age.* Rev. ed. Grand Rapids: Eerdmans, 1990.

Jorgenson, Allen G. "Authenticating Novelty." *Word and World* 26.2 (2006) 188–94.

———. "On the Art of Distinguishing Law from Law." In *Transformative Theological Perspectives,* Vol. 6, *Theology in the Life of the Church,* edited by Karen L. Bloomquist, 155–66. Minneapolis: Lutheran University Press, 2009.

Jüngel, Ebehard, and Karl Rahner. *Was ist ein Sakrament?* Freibrug, Germany: Herder, 1971.

King, Thomas. *The Truth about Stories: A Native Narrative.* Toronto: Anansi, 2003.

Kolb, Robert, and Timothy J. Wengert. *The Book of Concord: The Confessions of the Evangelical Lutheran Church.* Minneapolis: Fortress, 2000.

Luther, Martin. *D. Martin Luthers Werke: Kritische Gesamtausgabe, 5 Band.* Weimar: Hermann Böhlau, 1892.

———. "On the Bondage of the Will (1525)." In *Career of the Reformer 3*, Vol. 33, *Luther's Works,* edited by Philip S. Watson and Helmut T. Lehman, translated by Philip S. Watson and Benjamin Drewery, 3–295. Philadelphia: Fortress, 1972.

———. "The Sacrament of the Body and Blood of Christ—Against the Fanatics (1526)." In *Word and Sacrament 2*, Vol. 36, *Luther's Works,* edited by Abdel Ross Wentz and Helmut T. Lehmann, translated by Frederick C. Ahrens, 329–61. Philadelphia: Fortress, 1959.

Meeks, M. Douglas. *God the Economist: The Doctrine of God and Political Economy.* Minneapolis: Fortress, 1989.

Metzger, Bruce M., and Roland E. Murphy, editors. *The New Oxford Annotated Bible with the Apocryphal/Deuterocanonical Books, New Revised Standard Version.* New York: Oxford University Press, 1991.

Nouwen, Henri. *The Spirituality of Fund-Raising.* New York: Upper Room Ministries/Henry Nouwen Society, 2004.

Palmer, Parker J. *The Courage to Teach: Exploring the Inner Landscape of a Teacher's Life.* San Francisco: Jossey-Bass, 1998.

Powell, Mark Allan. *Giving to God: The Bible's Good News about Living a Generous Life.* Grand Rapids: Eerdmans, 2006.

Rahner, Karl. *Spirit in the World.* Translated by William V. Dych. New York: Continuum, 1994.

Regan, Jane E. *Toward an Adult Church: A Vision of Faith Formation.* Chicago: Loyola, 2002.

Schleiermacher, Friedrich. *Dialectic; Or, the Art of Doing Philosophy: A Study Edition of the 1811 Notes.* Translated and edited by Terrence N. Tice. Atlanta: Scholars, 1996.

Senn, Frank C. *A Stewardship of the Mysteries.* New York: Paulist Press, 1999.

Tanner, Kathryn. *Economy of Grace.* Minneapolis: Fortress, 2005.

Taylor, Charles. *A Secular Age.* Cambridge: Harvard University Press, 2007.

———. *Sources of the Self: The Making of Modern Identity.* Cambridge: Harvard University Press, 1989.

Tinker, George E. *American Indian Liberation: A Theology of Sovereignty.* Maryknoll, NY: Orbis, 2008.

Truth and Reconciliation Canada. Winnipeg: Truth and Reconciliation Commission of Canada, Indian Residential Schools Settlement Agreement. No pages. Online: http://www.trc-cvr.ca/index_e.html.

Weil, Simone. *Waiting for God*. Translated by Emma Craufurd. New York: Harper & Row, 1951.

Wharton, J. A. "Stewards, Stewardship." In *The Interpreter's Dictionary of the Bible: An Illustrated Encyclopedia, Volume 4,* edited by George Arthur Buttrick, 443. Nashville: Abingdon, 1962.

Index

Aquinas. *See* Thomas Aquinas, Saint
Aristotle, 24n4
art, 93, 94, 96, 99
astonishment. *See* awe
awe
    and baptism, 1, 6–10
    bigger than any image, 119
    and education, 86, 87–89, 92, 95
    at existence, 97
    at gifts given, 10
    and gospel, 95
    and identity of steward, x, 1, 37, 46, 69, 101
    at meeting Christ, 37
    and mystery, 112
    and prayer, 49, 67
    and proclamation, 105, 107, 112
    in relationship to experience, 14–15

Bach, Johann Sebastian, 31
baptism
    See also word and sacrament
    conveys forgiveness, 63
    conveys vocation, 9
    daily return to, 7
    as death, 100, 117
    as eternal event, 7, 9
    as non-repeatable, 8
    points to astonishment, 8
    recalls world's genesis, 81
    and space, 7
    and teaching, 87–91, 97
    and time, 6–10
Barth, Karl, 6
Barzun, Jaques, 90n1, 91n4, 93n6
Beatitudes, 60
Body
    and ambiguity, 73, 74
    as described in Scripture, 73–74
    human as spirit in, 23
    as an instance of the world, 100
    and interdependence, 40
    of Christ. *See* church
    in platonic paradigm, 82
    politic, 23, 29
    and prayer, 66, 68
    proper, 69–75
    and world, 70–71
bread, 58, 61–62, 134

Calvin, John, 103

Christ
See also body of Christ *and* Jesus
alone, 30, 38–40
catholic body of and Eucharist, 12
Christians live in, 5, 8
and exchange, 20
gives words of Lord's Prayer, 56
history centered in, 8
and hypostatic union, 39
informs fundraising, 40, 47
institutes the sacraments, 8
inverts human project, 17
and justification, 16
and kenosis, 102, 108
meets Christian in vulnerability, 28
as only priest, 89
as our Rabbi, 90
present in sacramental act of the church, 4, 13
promises presence within church, 7
self communication of God in, 14
as steward, 21
time anticipates, 8
Christology, 38, 39
Church
and education, 102
exists
as a body, 76
as body of Christ, 3
as citizen of body politic, 26
and Lord' Prayer, 56
and mission, 83
and ordination, 77–80
politics as part and parcel of, 4, 39
practices of, ix, x, 1
receives to give, 15
three moments in life of, 6
and world, 83–85
common priesthood. *See* priesthood of all believers
communication
mysterious nature of, 51
organic paradigm, 108–9
technical paradigm, 107–8
variety of, 54
Communion, Holy, 81, 106
See also Eucharist
confirmation, 88, 101
creation
and ambiguity, 74
anticipates redemption, 42, 81, 84
and body, 75
and Christian service, 43, 74, 113
evidences grace, 97
and God's action, 18
and language, 50

creation (cont.),
   and law, 42n6
   made new, 16, 22, 37, 81
   and redemption reflect grace, 107
   seen through Scripture, 40–42, 50, 103–4
cross alone, 39–43
culture, 29, 35, 39, 82, 103, 104
curiosity, 37, 95, 96–104

death, 11, 65–6, 99–100, 105, 117
Dillard, Annie, 36, 37n4

economist, 18–9, 23
economy
   modern, 23–24
   of reversal, 43
   practices of early world, 4, 19, 22
   and Trinity, 17, 84
eternity, 9, 12, 36, 60
Eucharist
   See also word and sacrament
   and Christ's presence, 89
   and forgiveness, 63
   informs stewardship, 14
   makes a space sacred, 12
   paradigmatic event of thanksgiving, 47
   points to expectation, 1, 8, 104
   points to world's consummation, 81, 110–11
   and preaching, 88, 104
   and reception of word of God, 105–6
   and space, 10–13
   and time, 7
evil, 31–32, 42–43, 65, 66–67, 114
expectation
   bigger than any image, 119
   and education, 86, 87, 92, 95, 96
   and Eucharist, 1, 6, 8, 10–13, 104
   and gospel, 35
   and identity of steward, x, 1, 37, 46, 68, 101
   and mystery, 112
   and prayer, 49, 55
   and proclamation, 105–7, 112
   and space, 13
   in relationship to awe, 14–15

faith
   alone, 30, 34, 45–48
   and grace, 16, 28, 112
   as mode of knowledge, 72
   and nescience, 100
   and prayer, 68
   in relationship to education, 91–92
   and sacraments, 8
First Nations, 101–2
forgiveness, 62–63, 105

fundraising
    and community, 34
    as divine possibility, 47
    as fund-seeing, 38
    and interdependence, 40
    as a spiritual gift, 33
    spirituality of, 32–34
    theology of, 34–38

Good Samaritan, 95
Gospel
    allows failure, 28
    authority is kenotic, 43
    and church, 27
    and gifts, 32, 33, 40
    habit of hearing, 35
    and justice, 29
    and justification, 27
    and law, 42, 55
    and money, 30, 32, 47, 115
    and mystery, 5
    and ordination, 78, 80, 90
    preaching of, 105, 106
    proclaimed in entire worship service, 110
    in relationship to creation, 41, 103
    and Scripture, 43, 44
    stewards of, 6, 15, 53, 59, 86, 91
    stewardship of, 15, 104, 106
    teaching of, 87, 88, 91
grace
    alone, 34–38
    awakens us, 36
    children of God by, 21, 22
    creates awe and expectation, 9, 46
    creates receptive hearts, 45
    and creation, 97
    and faith, 16, 28, 112
    makes us response-able, 107
    mystery of, 112
    orders prayer, 55
    and ordination, 80, 89
    plenitude of, 9, 10, 84
    and prayer, 55, 68
    and sacraments, 8, 13, 78, 116
    saved by, 7, 16
    and teaching, 96
Great Commission, 85, 97, 91, 104

Hall, Douglas John, ix
heaven, 57–58, 59–60
Holy Spirit
    bears Word, 18
    and body, 74
    and Father and Son, 18, 21, 57, 58, 88
    fundraising as gift of, 40
    gift of, 17
    and Magnificat, 28
    and prayer, 52–53
    and spiritual gifts, 34
    and teaching, 86, 87

Index

idolatry, 113–14
image of Christ, 17
image of God, 41–42
Indigenous Canadians, *See* First Nations
intuition, 93–94
Israel, 39, 61, 74

Jesus
    See also Christ
    alone, 30, 38–40
    does not try us, 65
    encountered in learning, 102
    fully human, fully divine, 38, 39
    inverts the human project, 17, 19
    is our justice, 22
    is our Rabbi, 90
    and justification, 16
    and kenosis, 107
    and money, 31, 44, 115
    prayer of, 55–68
    presence of, 3, 10–12
    as priest, 89
    as primordial sacrament, 2
    as teacher, 86
Jorgenson, Allen G., 36n2, 42n6
Jüngel, Eberhard, 2
justice
    a difficult concept, 24
    an eschatological category, 25
    and fair play, 23
    and good of the world, 23
    and injustice, 24, 56, 102
    Jesus is our, 22
    and justification, 27, 29
    stewards of, 22–29
justification
    as God's conversion of the human project, 16, 17
    and incorporation in Christ, 21
    in relationship to justice, 27–29
    and stewardship, 15, 17–21, 27–29
    and Trinity, 21, 29
    and word and sacrament, 27

kairos, 8n7, 11
kenosis, 77, 102, 107, 108–9, 111
King, Thomas, 102n11

law, 24, 42, 55
Lord's Supper, *See* Eucharist
love
    engenders love, 14
    expansive character of, 117
    God's love for world, 44, 81, 83, 103,
    kenotic character of, 46
    and money, 31
    and neighbours, 100

love (cont.),
    overflows in reign of God, 14
    and stewardship, 24
    suffering, 60
    and Trinity, 18
Luther, Martin, 7, 9, 16, 19, 30n1, 41, 42, 55, 60n9, 61, 65, 66, 82, 88, 89, 105, 106

Magnificat, 28, 58
Meeks, M. Douglas, 18n1
money
    and evil, 32
    flows through church, 116
    and gospel, 30
    and idolatry, 113
    integral to God's mission, 44
    as part of community's story, 43
    phenomenon of, 30
    as power, 40
    and prayer, 49
    and proclamation, 44
    as stand in, 23, 31
    theology of, 131–32
    as a tool of communication, 45–46
mystery, 3, 5–6, 47, 49, 92, 101, 108, 111–12, 117

new birth, 13, 14
Native Canadians, *See* First Nations

Nouwen, Henri, 44
novelty, 35

oikonomos, 4
ordination, 5, 77–80, 88–90, 106

Palmer, Parker, 90n2, 91, 94n9
parable, 3, 44, 58, 85, 95
Picasso, Pablo, 93
place. *See* space
Plato, 73, 97
politics, 38–40, 44, 82
power, 21, 31–32, 43, 47, 80, 115, 117
prayer
    and change, 52–67
    as gift and task, 50–53
    Lord's Prayer, 55–68
    as means of communication, 50, 54–55
    as primordial speech, 51
    and stewardship, 9, 49–54, 116
priesthood of all believers, 5, 77–80, 89–90, 106, 115
preaching. *See* proclamation
proclamation
    in broad and narrow sense, 14, 76
    as children's sermons, 103–4
    and church in the world, 84
    content is grace, 35–36

proclamation (cont.),
　depends upon preacher's listening, 111
　and Eucharist, 88, 105–6
　as instantiation of stewardship, 11
　mystery revealed by, 5
　of stewardship, 113–17
　stewardship of, 106–13
　a symphonic event, 44
　as a trialogue, 107
promise, 7, 13–4, 42, 47, 55, 89
Pym, Jeff, xi, 118

Rahner, Karl, 2n1, 70
Reagan, Jane, 92n5, 96
reign of God
　expanded by love, 117
　grasps us in sermon, 111
　and human agency, 47, 72
　and Lord's Prayer
　　and daily bread, 62
　　as inversion of life, 58–59
　　and sin's continuance, 66
　made stewards for, 17
　mystery of, 112
　and plenitude, 111
　politics not excluded, 39
　prayer makes us available for, 68
　and reign of heavens, 57
　and rest in heaven, 60

resurrection, 17, 19, 67, 72, 108

sacraments. *See* word and sacrament
salvation
　described in plurality of tenses, 7
　event character of, 6
　and Lord's Prayer, 56
　as reorientation of eyes, 37
Schleiermacher, Friedrich, 93n7
Scripture
　alone, 30, 43–45
　and body, 73, 74
　and inheritance metaphor, 20
　as lens, 103
　narrates relationship between creation and redemption, 41
　and prayer, 49, 61
　and stewardship metaphor, 20
　and world, 81, 83
senses, 97–98
sin, 29, 41, 42, 60, 63–66, 73, 80, 83, 88
space
　and divine promise, 7
　and Eucharist, 10–13
　location of events, 7
　profane, 11, 12
　reconfigured, 10
　sacred, 11, 12

Index

space (cont.),
   and time, 11–13, 60
   two modes of, 11
steward
   as agents of reconciliation, 116
   birthed not made, 5
   exists bodily, 72, 74, 75
   as expectant, 13
   are gifted, 13, 33, 34
   God as, 19
   God works through, 32
   of justice, 16, 22–27
   live by promise, 14
   more than, 17–21, 118, 119
   of the body of Christ, 75–81
   of the mysteries, 4–5
   of proclamation, 106–13
   of time, talents, and treasures, 114
   and prayer
    in general, 53–55
       and Lord's Prayer, 55–68
   refusal of identity as idolatry, 99, 114
   as shaped by the gospel, 15
   translates economist, 18
   and world, 81–85
stewardship
   and ancient household, 20
   bestowed on servants of the gospel, 6
   committees, 116
   and fundraising, 30, 32–48
   grounded in word and sacrament, 116
   and inheritance, 20–21
   inverted by God as steward, 19
   and justice, 22–28
   and justification, 17–21, 27–29
   as metaphor, 15, 22
   month, 115
   and obligation, 118
   of body
       identified as world, 74, 81–85
   of Christ, 75–80
       proper, 69–74
   as opposed to idolatry, 113
   and prayer
       as commanded to pray always, 49–54
       Lord's Prayer, 55–68
       as vocation, 67
       with two eyes, 67
   and proclamation
       as preaching, 106–17
       sermon as instantiation of, 111
   project and process paradigms of, 115–17
   and risk, 107
   and sacrament, 1, 2–13
       of baptism, 6–10

stewardship
and sacrament (cont.),
of Eucharist, 10–13
as singular task of the
church, 78
and speech, 52–53
and teaching, 86, 96–103
theology of, ix, 1
vital signs of, ix

talent. *See* time, talents and
treasure
Taylor, Charles, 26, 27n6,
84n6, 94n8
teaching
and baptism, 87
and church, 102
and fear, 99–100
invokes vulnerability, 90
is preaching the gospel,
87
and learning, 86, 91–96
as a mystery, 90
and nescience, 98–99
as part of the *missio Dei*,
91
and preaching, 87–91
and residential schools,
101–2
technology, 35, 81, 84–85
temptation. *See* trial
Thomas Aquinas, Saint,
60n8, 61, 63, 66
time
awareness of, 36
and baptism, 6–10
chronos and *kairos*, 11

end of, 63
mundane experience
of, 62
reconfigured in Christ,
8, 10
and space, 11–13, 60
as stillness, 36
talents and treasure, 30,
32, 53, 54, 106, 107,
114
versus eternity, 60, 94
Tinker, George E., 102n11
treasure. *See* time, talents
and treasure
trial, 29, 46, 63–65, 65n17
Trinity
and baptism, 88
and economy, 18
immanent and eco-
nomic, 17–18
See also Christ, Holy
Spirit, Jesus

vocation, 9, 43, 44, 50, 67,
83, 84

Weil, Simone, 62
word and sacrament
as bookends of the
church, 1
as center of church, 13,
76
as Christ's presence, 4
engender a posture of
awe and expectation,
28
form Christians, 14

word and sacrament (cont.),
    ground stewardship, 116
    illumined by stewardship, 119
    and justification, 27, 29
    and knowledge, 72
    and Lord's Prayer, 56
    and mystery, 6
    and ordination, 78, 89
    as stewardship's vital signs, 18
world
    and being human, 23, 45–46, 54, 70–71, 73
    and church, 40, 80, 83–85, 101
    in contrast to reign of God, 43
    as established by God, 41, 51n2
    God's love for, 44, 81
    God's will for, 56, 57, 67
    and knowing, 98, 100
    and mission, 44, 76
    stewardship of, 81–85
    variously portrayed in Scripture, 73, 74
worship, 70, 110, 115, 116

www.ingramcontent.com/pod-product-compliance
Lightning Source LLC
Chambersburg PA
CBHW072150160426
43197CB00012B/2318